*TWAYNE'S WORLD AUTHORS SERIES*

*A Survey of the World's Literature*

# FRANCE

Maxwell A. Smith, Guerry Professor of French, Emeritus
The University of Chattanooga
Former Visiting Professor in Modern Languages
The Florida State University

EDITOR

*Mademoiselle de Scudéry*

TWAS 441

Mademoiselle de Scudéry

# MADEMOISELLE DE SCUDÉRY

By NICOLE ARONSON

*East Carolina University*

Translated by
STUART R. ARONSON

TWAYNE PUBLISHERS

A DIVISION OF G. K. HALL & CO., BOSTON

**Library of Congress Cataloging in Publication Data**
Aronson, Nicole.
  Mademoiselle de Scudéry.
  (Twayne's world authors series ; TWAS 441)
  Bibliography: p. 171–174
  Includes index.
  1. Scudéry, Madeleine de, 1607–1701. 2. Authors,
French—17th century—Biography. I. Title.
PQ1922.Z5A83    843'.4[B]    78-1413
ISBN 0-8057-6278-7

To my Mother

# Contents

# *About the Author*

Nicole Aronson is currently Professor of Romance Languages and Literatures at East Carolina University. A native of Bordeaux (France), she received her License ès Lettres from the Faculté des Lettres of the University of Bordeaux, and earned a Ph.D. at the City University of New York. Prior to her present position she taught at Marymount College (Tarrytown, New York) and at the American University of Washington, D.C.

Dr. Aronson is the author of *Les Idées politiques de Rabelais*, published by Nizet (1973) and of several articles which have appeared in various journals such as *Romanische Forschungen, Studi Francesi,* and the *French Review.* At the present time she is collaborating on a book dealing with feminist problems as seen through female French writers, a subject in which she is highly interested.

# Preface

Few authors in the history of literature have known the greatest of renown and critical acclaim during their lifetimes only later to fall into a position of near oblivion and utter contempt. This is the case of Mlle de Scudéry, who, in modern times, has been regarded as an excessively prudish and bigoted old maid, and whose lengthy novels are considered unreadable and therefore not worthy of study. As a result, books concerning her life and work have been rare, and, indeed, the only one published in English appeared decades ago.

The situation was quite different in the seventeenth century. The novels of Mlle de Scudéry were at the top of the bestseller list, and they were read by everyone from Corneille to Mme de Lafayette and from Pascal to Mme de Sévigné. This alone is reason enough to rescue them from obscurity. How can we remain indifferent to material that once fascinated, and most likely influenced, many authors of the seventeenth century whom we now study so closely? Mlle de Scudéry, even today, is considered one of the most representative authors of *Préciosité*, a movement still not well known. Surely a study of *Préciosité* which does not deal with works that were read by all of the *Précieuses* and with which they closely identified themselves would certainly be strangely incomplete.

Her lengthy works—namely, *Ibrahim, Cyrus*, and *Clélie*—which delighted those of Corneille's generation, followed the style of the heroic novel that was so popular during the first half of the century. This was a time of the kind of heroic action that was typified by *Le Cid*. When Louis XIV took the throne a change in taste and mentality had begun to take place that caused this type of heroic deed to eventually disappear. At the same time the long epic novel gave way to the much shorter *nouvelle*. Mlle de Scudéry was sensitive to the change, and after 1661 she wrote *Célinte, Mathilde*, and *La Promenade de Versailles*, all in the new style. Her last works, the series of *Conversations morales*, were in the same vein as the moralistic preoccupations that inspired La Rochefoucauld and La Bruyère. These volumes, written in a most vivacious way, allow us a rather penetrating insight into Mlle de Scudéry's intimate philosophical beliefs as well as her literary tastes.

Mlle de Scudéry therefore has a great deal to offer the reader who refuses to be discouraged by the imposing number of volumes that she has left us. He has the opportunity of making the acquaintance of an extraordinarily cultured woman who has a sense of humor for which she is generally not given credit, as well as a keen awareness of the changes in the literary tastes of her century. In reflecting these changes her career can be said to summarize, in many ways, the literary evolution of the seventeenth century.

NICOLE ARONSON

*East Carolina University*

# *Acknowledgments*

I wish to acknowledge the invaluable aid in research I have found in Rathery and Boutron's *Mademoiselle de Scudéry,* and in Georges Mongrédien's "Bibliographie des oeuvres de Georges et Madeleine de Scudéry."

I am especially grateful to M. Jacques Yvon, director of the Bordeaux Public Library, without whose assistance this work might never have been completed.

I must also thank the East Carolina University Research Council; Mrs. Marguerite A. Perry, chairperson of the Department of Foreign Languages and Literatures, East Carolina University; Mrs. Mary Frances Morris, reference librarian, East Carolina University; Dr. Robert Nunn of Bowdoin College; Mr. Gunter Strumpf of East Carolina University; and Miss Martha Culton. I also wish to acknowledge the special help given me by Dr. Joseph A. Fernandez of East Carolina University.

With the exception of quotations from sources written in English, everything has been translated from French by Stuart Aronson.

# Chronology

1644    Georges and Madeleine de Scudéry travel to Rouen to settle certain family matters.

1644    December: Georges de Scudéry, accompanied by his sister, travels to Marseille to assume his post.

1647    They return to Paris, where Madeleine de Scudéry continues to live with her brother after she fails to obtain the position of educating Mazarin's three nieces.

1649    Madeleine de Scudéry takes the side of Voiture in the dispute concerning Voiture's *Sonnet d'Uranie* and Benserade's *Sonnet de Job*.

1648    The *Fronde*. Madeleine de Scudéry spends this period in
1652    Paris. Despite her relationship with the Condé family, she takes no part in the rebellion and remains loyal to the crown.

1649    Publication of the ten volumes of *Artamène ou Le Grand*
1653    *Cyrus* under the name of Georges de Scudéry. Despite the political situation, during which the Condé family was generally in disfavor with the crown, each volume is dedicated to Mme de Longueville, Condé's sister.

1650    Georges de Scudéry is elected to the *Académie française* where he replaces Vaugelas.

1653    Georges and Madeleine de Scudéry establish residence in Rue de Beauce at the corner of Rue des Oiseaux. It is here that the *Samedis* encounters begin, at which time Paul Pellisson establishes a close relationship with Mlle de Scudéry that will last until his death.

1653    December 20: *Journée des Madrigaux*.

1654    Publication of the ten volumes of *Clélie, Histoire romaine*
1661    under the name of Georges de Scudéry.

1654    Georges and Madeleine de Scudéry no longer live together. Being threatened with arrest because of his relationship with the Condé family during the *Fronde*, Georges flees to Granville, a city near Le Hâvre, where he marries on June 14, 1654. His wife is Marie-Madeleine de Montcal de Martinvast, twenty-seven years of age and a passionate devotee of novels.

1656    The dispute in regard to Raincy's madrigal, which Ménage falsely says was copied from Tasso.. Everyone takes sides, including Mme de Rambouillet, but Mlle de Scudéry is the only one to recognize that it was merely a hoax perpetrated by Ménage.

1656    Pellisson and Ménage publish works by Sarasin. The book is dedicated to Mlle de Scudéry and the permission to publish is signed by Conrart. It has been said that this could be considered a manifesto of the *Précieux.*

1657    Paul Pellisson has won the confidence of Fouquet, the royal administrator of finances, and becomes his secretary. Madeleine de Scudéry receives a pension from Fouquet and is a frequent guest at his various residences.

1658    Publication of *Almahide ou L'Esclave-Reine* under the name of Georges de Scudéry; this novel, written with his wife, is the only one in which Mlle de Scudéry played no role.

1659    Gilles Boileau is elected to the *Académie française,* an election against which Mlle de Scudéry and Pellisson campaigned vigorously.

1659    November 18: Production of Molière's *Les Précieuses ridicules.*

1660    August 17: *Fétes de Vaux,* attended by Mlle de Scudéry.

1661    *Célinte, Nouvelle première* published anonymously.

1661    November: Fouquet and his secretary Pellisson are imprisoned by order of the king.

1666    January 16: Pellisson is released from the Bastille and will eventually regain the favor of the king. Fouquet does not obtain his release and dies at Pignerol in 1680.

1666(?)The onset of the deafness that will oblige Mlle de Scudéry, at the end of her life, to communicate in writing.

1667    *Mathilde d'Aguilar,* published anonymously.

1667    May 14: Georges de Scudéry dies.

1669    Mlle de Scudéry visits Versailles and writes *La Promenade de Versailles,* dedicated to the king, and published anonymously. Included in this volume is the short story "Célanire."

1670    October: Paul Pellisson converts to Catholicism.

1671    The *Académie française* awards Mlle de Scudéry the first prize for her *Discours de la gloire.* It is the first time that the prize, founded by Balzac, is awarded.

1680    *Conversations sur divers sujets,* in two volumes, published anonymously. Volume II includes "Les Bains des Thermopyles."

1684    *Conversations nouvelles sur divers sujets,* in two volumes, dedicated to the king, and published anonymously. Volume II includes "L'Histoire du Comte d'Albe."

1684    Mlle de Scudéry is elected to the Academy dei Ricovrati of Padua.

1686    *Conversations morales,* in two volumes, published anonymously, and dedicated to the king.

1688    *Nouvelles conversations de morale,* in two volumes, dedicated to the king, and published anonymously.

1692    *Entretiens de Morale,* in two volumes, dedicated to the king, and published anonymously.

1693    Paul Pellisson dies.

1701    June 2: Mlle de Scudéry dies in Paris and is buried at her parish church, Saint-Nicolas des Champs. Her death is announced in *La Gazette* and *Le Mercure de France.*

# CHAPTER 1

# The Life of Mlle de Scudéry

## I  Authorship

WHEN the de Scudérys spoke of their family misfortunes one could have believed, as Tallemant des Réaux has pointed out,[1] that they were speaking about the fall of the Roman Empire. Although the events they were referring to were evidently not nearly as earth-shattering, the de Scudéry family had indeed seen better days. It is not known for certain if it had its origin in Italy, as may be supposed owing to the similarity between Scudéry and the Italian "Scudiere,"[2] but there is documentation that the de Scudéry family was living in Apt, a small city in the south of France, as early as the fourteenth century.

Toward the end of the sixteenth century Georges de Scudéry left his native Apt in the service of Georges de Brancas, Sieur de Villars. Brancas was eventually named admiral of France and filled the post of governor at Le Hâvre. It was here that Georges de Scudéry was appointed captain of the port, married, and had five children. Two of them, Georges and Madeleine, survived infancy. When Brancas left his post as governor, this signaled the beginning of bad times for Georges de Scudéry, who was even imprisoned for a short while, and when he died in 1613 his young children found themselves in a most difficult situation.

As soon as he was of age, Georges de Scudéry, the son, undertook a military career that seems to have had some brilliant moments. Because of his boasting and arrogance he is often badly judged and, as a result, his true value is not always fully appreciated. The fact is, however, that he was considered by many to be both a fine soldier and a brilliant writer. Turenne, one of the greatest generals of the seventeenth century, admired him and is quoted as having said: "I would gladly trade all that I have done for de Scudéry's retreat at the

Pass of Suse."[3] This was undoubtedly a remarkable tribute to his prowess as a soldier. After 1630 he abandoned his military career to dedicate himself to dramatic literature. Here too he was extremely successful, and Balzac, for example, confessed to having preferred de Scudéry's *L'Amour tyrannique* to Corneille's *Le Cid*.[4] In 1642, through the influence of Mme de Rambouillet, he obtained the post of governor of Notre-Dame-de-la-Garde in Marseille, and also held the position of captain of the royal galleys.

Most likely Madeleine and Georges de Scudéry exaggerated the nobility of their birth, but this fact does have its importance. It seems to be one of the reasons that led Mlle de Scudéry to cloak herself in anonymity. As a result, none of her work was published in her own name during her lifetime. With the exception of *Célinte* and *Mathilde d'Aguilar*, her brother's name, while he was alive, appeared as the author. When he died she published anonymously, but it is notable that later editions of *Conversations* printed in Amsterdam did bear her name, and that the *faux-titre* of *Conversations morales* of 1686 carried the inscription "by M. de S.D.R."[5] Of course it was a secret known to all that Madeleine de Scudéry, even before *Cyrus*, was her brother's collaborator, if not the sole author of the novels credited to him. Tallemant once again tells us that "she wrote a part of *Les Femmes illustres* and all of *L'Illustre Bassa*."[6] In regard to the rest of the novels, Georges de Scudéry wrote the prefaces and the long, formal letter of dedication that were in fashion at the time, but the authorship of these books was well known. Evidence of this can be readily seen in Furetière's allusion to the famous key to the characters in *Cyrus*, which circulated widely and which indicated from whom these characters were drawn in real life. For example, the hero Cyrus was none other than Condé, and Mandane, Mme de Longueville. Furetière pointed out that it was necessary to add this to the key: "M. de Scudéry. . . . *Mademoiselle sa soeur*."[7]

It must be said, however, that in this novel, with its abundance of military campaigns, the participation of Georges de Scudéry seems quite evident. We assume this because the battles are retraced with great technical precision, and this information was available only in documents belonging to the Condé library.[8] It was not until long after the publication of *Cyrus* that these documents were made public. It is not difficult to imply from this that Georges de Scudéry,

with a soldier's curiosity, availed himself of the material and inserted it in the novel.

In her correspondence with friends, Madeleine de Scudéry
openly acknowledged the authorship of the novels. In a letter sent
to her in 1650, the poet Sarasin, writing at the request of Mme de
Longueville, thanked her for having forwarded the fifth volume of
*Cyrus*. Sarasin, who is portrayed in *Clélie* as the gallant Amilcar,
was a great friend of Madeleine de Scudéry, and knowing precisely
what the situation was, thanked her for her *Cyrus* and included a
word of appreciation for her brother's preface (R. 128–31). We
clearly see that Sarasin was in complete agreement with Tallemant:
the sister wrote the novels, with the occasional assistance of her
brother, who was entrusted with the prefaces and letters of
dedication.

It is tempting to try to understand the reasons for Mlle de Scudéry's desire for anonymity. Tallemant, gossip that he often was,
said that Georges de Scudéry signed his sister's work so that it
would sell better. This is a possibility when one considers how well
known he was as a result of his plays and his participation in the
*Querelle du Cid*. Another reason was indicated by Tallemant. Love
was a frequently mentioned subject in the novels, and a female
author would run the risk of severe criticism by the sanctimonious,
who believed that "such a subject was less pardonable when written
by a woman."[9] Boileau, in his *Dialogue des Héros de roman*, attacked Mlle de Scudéry after her death for this very reason.[10]
Perhaps, however, the most probable explanation can be discerned
from a statement made by one of Mlle de Scudéry's heroines,
Sapho, the Greek poetess: "There is nothing more unpleasant than
to be a woman of letters and be treated as one when one is of noble
birth" (*Cyrus*, X, 366). She goes on to say: "I only wish to be like
everybody else." Actually, the portrait of Sapho is Mlle de Scudéry
herself, both physically and morally. It is necessary to note, however, that while she was referred to in her circle as Sapho, this is
simply an allusion to the literary glory of the Greek poetess and not
to her amorous tastes. Many poets of the time gave tribute in their
poems to Sapho–Mlle de Scudéry, and wrote of the love that she
had inspired in them.

This reluctance to play the role of the woman of letters that Mlle
de Scudéry ascribes to Sapho may very well be the best explanation

for her own attitude, and it is interesting to note that Mme de Lafayette, too, was unwilling to be thought of as a writer.[11] Reluctant as she was at first to accept the notoriety that naturally came from being the author of best-selling novels, Mlle de Scudéry eventually resigned herself to accepting the situation because of financial exigencies.

Whatever assets that had been left to Georges and Madeleine de Scudéry were dispensed by Georges, and he seems to have run through everything. He was an avid collector of unusual objects, and also possessed a beautiful collection of paintings and etchings, notably works by Dürer, Bruegel, and Callot.[12] Naturally, their financial situation had been greatly affected by Georges's *fantaisies de collectionneur,* and when Mlle de Scudéry began living alone, in 1654, she admitted having difficulty at times in making ends meet. However, her renown as a writer enabled her to receive gifts and pensions that, while not always paid, allowed her, nevertheless, a certain amount of independence.[13]

Among her benefactors were Mazarin, Fouquet, Queen Christina of Sweden, Louis XIV, the Bishop of Münster, and several rich friends whose help was in the form of practical gifts. For example, Mme du Plessis-Guénégaud completely furnished a room in her house, and Eléonore de Rohan-Montbazon, abbess of Malnoue, gave her a timepiece, an object quite rare in the seventeenth century. She also received, from time to time, jewels, rare plants, unusual animals, expensive fabrics, valuable paintings, and other equally sumptuous presents.

These, however, were not the only acknowledgements of her great stature as an author. She also was awarded the first prize in eloquence by the *Académie française* for her discourse on *La Gloire,* and was also elected to the Academy dei Ricovrati of Padua, upon the death of Elena Cornaro. If one is to believe Ménage, Mlle de Scudéry was even considered, at the time, for entry at the *Académie française* (R. 121), an honor not yet given to any woman. Unfortunately, the question was never resolved.

It seems quite plausible now to assume that Mlle de Scudéry's refusal to allow her name to appear on the cover of the most widely read novels of her time was not the result of modesty but stemmed rather from her conviction that a lady of noble birth just simply did not launch herself upon the literary scene. Nevertheless, she was undoubtedly the author of the novels that were the delight of the *Précieux* and which, according to Antoine Adam, were the ultimate expression of *Préciosité*.[14]

## II  *Youth*

The reversals in fortune that plagued the de Scudéry family did not end with the death of Georges de Scudéry the elder in 1613. His marriage with Madeleine de Martel de Goutimesnil resulted in five children, two of which survived infancy: Georges, baptized on August 12, 1601 and Madeleine, born, according to tradition, on November 15, 1607, and baptized on December 1, 1608 (this verified by baptismal records of Notre-Dame of Le Hâvre).[15] The death of their father, followed not long after by that of their mother, left them in a difficult situation. Luckily enough the young Madeleine was taken in by an uncle who had frequented the courts of three kings, and who was now living in the country, where he raised her with great care.

The details of Mlle de Scudéry's youth are not well known, and what little we do know comes mainly from the *Mémoires* of Valentin Conrart, in whom Mlle de Scudéry confided. Conrart,[16] the founder of the *Académie française*, was quite wealthy, and lived a comfortable life, surrounded by his many friends. He would see them either in the salons, at the Hôtel de Rambouillet, or receive them at his country house at Athis-sur-Mons, near Paris. It was in these lovely surroundings that Mlle de Scudéry passed many pleasurable hours. Her friendship with Conrart and his wife was very close. According to tradition, Conrart may have had stronger feelings for "Sapho," and is supposed to have been jealous of the men that associated with her. It is more than likely that the affection he felt for her certainly colored his description of her youth, but since it is the only document we have, the *Mémoires* cannot be overlooked:

Her uncle had her learn the skills and arts that were suitable for a girl of her age and situation, namely writing, spelling, dancing, drawing, painting, and other areas of endeavor. But beside the things she was taught, because of her prodigious imagination, her excellent memory, her acute judgement, her vivacious personality, and her natural desire to learn about all she saw and all she heard that was worthwhile, she taught herself about things concerning agriculture, gardening, the running of a country household, and cooking. She also learned about the causes and effects of sicknesses, the composition of an infinite amount of remedies, about perfumes, toilet water, and distillations both useful and pleasurable. She had a desire to learn to play the lute and took some lessons with some success, but since it is an endeavor that demands a great deal of time, and the result is merely an amusement, she thought it best to employ her time in pursuits of a more intellectual nature. She often heard Italian and Spanish spoken, and was aware of the many books in both languages that were in her uncle's library, which he highly prized. This naturally led her to the study of these languages, and before long she succeeded so admirably in mastering both comprehension and pronunciation that no author was too difficult for her.[17]

Certain facts seem to be quite accurate, and Conrart was probably correct when he wrote of the great care taken in Mlle de Scudéry's education. Her spelling, for example, was remarkably correct at a time when this accomplishment was rare. A casual glance at the letters of Mme de Sévigné or of Mme de Lafayette is sufficient to realize just how precise Mlle de Scudéry was in comparison with those eminent women. She attached great importance to the proper use of language, and often encouraged women to learn to write an acceptable French. In *Cyrus*, she remarked that one scoffed at foreigners (the Scythians) who pronounced Greek (meaning French) badly, and she comments: "There is, however, much more reason to find it peculiar that an intelligent woman can make a thousand mistakes in writing her own language, than to find a Scythian who cannot speak Greek well" (X, 403).

Excellent spelling was but one aspect of Mlle de Scudéry's vast culture. She knew both Spanish and Italian, according to Conrart, but had not studied Latin. Ancient history, however, was far from unknown to her. In the preface to *Cyrus* she cited both Herodotus and Xenophon as sources, and commented on her approach to them: "At times I used one or the other according to how well they fitted my purposes." The eighth volume of *Clélie* contains the history of Hesiod in which Mlle de Scudéry, employing a technique found in epic poetry, has the Muse Calliope, in a dream, present all the great characters of Greek, Latin, Italian, and French literatures (pp. 799–870). In *L'Histoire du Comte d'Albe*, there is a detailed study of French poetry up until the time of Henry IV. In a letter writen in 1685 or 1686, she speaks of Sultan Suleiman whom she had "greatly admired in (her) youth" (R. 301). Her interest in this part of the world is even more clearly demonstrated in the four volumes of

*Ibrahim ou L'Illustre Bassa*, which takes place in Constantinople. In *Mathilde d'Aguilar* and *L'Histoire du Comte d'Albe* she deals with Spanish history, and throughout the ten volumes of the *Conversations* she displays an enormous amount of knowledge in both contemporary and ancient history, art, and literature. It seems, then, that Mlle de Scudéry had an eager and curious mind and that, judging from Conrart's *Memoires*, biased though they may be, her uncle provided her with a quite remarkable education for a woman of that time.

In a letter written to Huet answering his *Discours sur l'origine des romans*, which he had just placed at the beginning of the edition of *Zaide*, Mlle de Scudéry spoke of what she had read in her youth: "You have chosen precisely the novels that were the delight of my early youth. These novels, which were compatible with decency and honesty, gave me an idea of what good fiction should be. I am referring to *Théagène et Chariclée*, *Théogène et Charide*, and also *L'Astrée*. These are the true sources from which my mind has drawn the knowledge that has given me such happiness" (R. 294). In regard to her reading material, there is a humorous anecdote that Tallemant recounts about Mlle de Scudéry's confessor. Having taken a book away from her that he considered not in good taste for "such a young girl," he replaced it with another that, unfortunately for him, had some spicy passages that had been clearly marked. When Mlle de Scudéry teased him about it, he insisted that the marks were not his.[18] True or false, this story confirms, however, the latitude the young girl had in her reading material.

The freedom of her education had an extremely healthy effect on Mlle de Scudéry, whose nature was a happy one. What was most striking in her was her aptitude for happiness. As in the case of Mme de Sévigné, to whom Mme de Lafayette wrote "[j]oy is the natural state of your soul,"[19] Mlle de Scudéry also found delight in everything she did. In her *Conversations nouvelles sur divers sujets*, written when she was well into her seventies, she observed: "The joy of life is born of itself and those who have it need only to be in good health to find pleasure in everything" (I, 43). That Mlle de Scudéry was blessed with this attribute clearly evinced itself when she wrote about the joy of visiting her friends, the joy of conversation, the joy of having a garden where a songbird would faithfully return each year, the joy of reading, and, less obviously stated but clearly understood, the joy of writing.

The fact that Mlle de Scudéry was orphaned at an early age does not seem to have had an adverse effect on her. As a matter of fact, the parents in her novels were either not mentioned or were used, as was often the custom at the time, merely as instruments to further the plot. The fathers placed obstacles in the way of their children's love affairs and were generally fearful of losing their authority. The mothers were usually more understanding and helpful. An example of this can be found in *Clélie*, where Clélius, father of the young girl, and Porsenna, father of the young man she loves, are both opposed to their getting married. The mothers, on the other hand, are in favor of the match and willingly facilitate the wishes of their children.[20] It should also be pointed out that, not surprisingly, many of Mlle de Scudéry's heroines are raised by uncles after the death of their parents. This is the case of Sapho in *Cyrus*, Plotine in *Clélie*, and Célanire in *La Promenade de Versailles*, to mention only a few.

Apropos of family relatives, one can see that the portrait of Charaxe, Sapho's brother, most likely resembles Georges de Scudéry, and through this we might have a good idea of the relationship between brother and sister. "The brother's inclinations are doubtlessly quite different from those of his sister. This is not to say that he has no good qualities, but that he has many bad ones. In effect he is courageous, but it is the kind of courage that makes the bull more valiant than the deer. It is not the type of courage that one associates with generosity, and which is necessary in an honest man" (*Cyrus*, X, 336–337). This rather negative portrait is in agreement with what Tallemant has written of Georges de Scudéry, who was astonished with the "strange patience" of his sister.

After the death of her uncle, Mlle de Scudéry, according to Conrart, "believed that she would do better to go to Paris than to stay in Rouen," where she had lived several years and where she had enjoyed the company of many cultivated people. The fact is that, for reasons unknown, she went to Paris in 1637 to live with her brother and continued to do so until 1654. One can suppose that despite certain obvious weaknesses of character in her brother, especially his rather cavalier way of handling money, the association did have certain advantages. Through him, because of his celebrity as a playwright, she was introduced into the literary society, including a probably very modest entry to the Hôtel de Rambouillet, then in all its glory.

### III  *La Chambre bleue d'Arthénice*

Having taken up residence in the Marais, an elegant section of Paris where she lived until her death, Mlle de Scudéry became a regular of the salon of the renowned Arthénice, Catherine de Rambouillet. The salon was referred to as *la chambre bleue* because of the color of the walls. Today the "Temple of Rue Saint-Thomas-du-Louvre," has become legendary as a veritable center of elegance and good taste. There is no question that Mme de Rambouillet did play an important role in the development of the "polite society" and in reforming the use of language, but it is necessary to remember that the principal reason she created the salon was for her own amusement. In a letter to Godeau, Chapelain pointed out that "the gallantry of the Hôtel de Rambouillet serves mainly as an amusement for Arthénice, of which she has great need."[21]

A stereotyped image of the Hôtel de Rambouillet tends to distort the true atmosphere that prevailed in this so frequently attended salon. It has been recently said that "the Malherbian cage suited the Hôtel de Rambouillet very well. Freedom of expression was going out of style, not only in poetry but in ideas, in manners, even in dress."[22] It is true that Mme de Rambouillet demanded a certain refinement of her guests, but, above all, a lively imagination seems to have been the main prerequisite for admission to the circle. In effect, she had the task of entertaining a group that consisted mainly of idlers who demanded a variety of spectacles, games, dinners, and amusing conversations, and this points to the importance of the search for novelty rather than to a demand for conformity. Antoine Adam reinforces this idea when he writes: "The Hôtel is, above all, a place where one has fun."[23]

In regard to the impression that the Hôtel entertained mainly aristocrats, this, too, is rather questionable. Of course, the presence of Voiture was generally excused because he was considered the official "jester," but he brought with him Mme Saintot, his mistress, the widow of a process server. Chevry, a boisterous businessman, Godeau, Gombault, Chapelain, Ménage, Conrart, and others with names equally bourgeois were all part of the group. Added to this quite unaristocratic array was the presence of some eminently undistinguished poets, among which was Neufgermain,[24] whose poems dedicated to Mme de Rambouillet are remembered more for their absurdity than for their elegance. Even if his presence was tolerated as a source of amusement, it is true that he was a constant guest at the Hôtel, and that he wrote numerous poems dedicated to Mme de Rambouillet, to her husband, and to their daughter, Julie d'Angennes.[25]

There is numerous mention of the many practical jokes that the guests of the Hôtel played on each other, and they were often not in the best of taste. Emile Magne tells us that "Mme de Rambouillet loved to trick even the most intimate of her friends, and as accomplice to Voiture she held her own when it came to exchanging jibes. Nothing could stop her when she felt the need to laugh."[26] Quite often one makes the mistake of associating the Hôtel de Rambouillet exclusively with the insipid poetry of *La Guirlande de Julie*, and forgets that the naughty poems of Voiture, namely *Sur sa maîtresse rencontrée en habit de garçon un soir de Carnaval*, or *A une demoiselle qui avait les manches de sa chemise retroussées et sales* or, worse yet, *A La Dame qui avait versé*[27] were all admired by the Hôtel.

However, side by side with Voiture and other middle class guests of the Hôtel de Rambouillet were many illustrious personages, such as the Condé entourage and certain distinguished writers. Mlle de Scudéry made the acquaintance of all and established lifelong friendships with a large number of these *habitués de la Chambre bleue*. It was also there, or perhaps at Mme de Sablé's salon, that she met Mlle Paulet, called the "lioness" because of her hot temper and flaming red hair. Mlle Paulet was a superb singer, and though living a pious life at the time, had once been known for her promiscuity. Mlle de Scudéry has depicted her life, although strongly censured, in *Cyrus*. Some of the correspondence between these two women has survived, and it clearly indicates the depth of their friendship, which began soon after Mlle de Scudéry's arrival in Paris and continued until Mlle Paulet's death during the *Fronde*.

It is indeed difficult to reconcile the traditional portrait of Mlle de Scudéry as being a bluestocking, a prude, and a bigot with the fact that she was so readily accepted into a society that evidently abhorred this type of person. One must remember that she was from the country, and already of an age that was considered, in the seventeenth century, no longer young. In order to compensate for this we can be sure that she had certain qualities that were quite attractive to the "regulars" in rue Saint-Thomas-du-Louvre.

It is generally accepted that *Cyrus* reflected the activities of the Hôtel de Rambouillet and its guests. Therefore we are able, through volume ten, to see how Mlle de Scudéry pictured herself. Since her literary portrait of Sapho was not disputed by her contemporaries, we can assume that it was an accurate one. It is not to be discounted, however, that, as Jean Rousset has noted, the literary self-portrait does leave itself open to certain doubts as to its complete veracity.[28] Here, to begin with, is a physical description that, despite a certain reticence, tells us that she was not pretty.

Even if she admits to being small in stature, not wanting to speak well of herself, she actually is of middling height. But being of noble aspect and having a pleasant figure, there is little more to desire. As for her coloring, it is not what one would consider fashionably white, but it is of such a luster that one could say it is beautiful. However, Sapho's ultimate physical quality is the beauty of her eyes. They are so lively, so loving, and so full of wit that it is at once difficult to hold their gaze and yet impossible to look away from them. (*Cyrus* X, 332)

To sum up, Mlle de Scudéry most likely had beautiful, lively eyes and a complexion that was rather dark. Mme Cornuel, one of the wittiest women of the seventeenth century, said rather unkindly that "since she had messed up so much paper, God made her sweat ink."[29] Even Chapelain, a good friend, complained of her homeliness: "She would be perfect except for being so ugly."[30] Although the Nanteuil portrait of Mlle de Scudéry has unfortunately been lost, there is one by Elisabeth Chéron that verifies the fact that she was, indeed, not physically attractive.

However, her intellectual qualities more than compensated for her lack of physical beauty. Even though she was extremely cultured, she detested pedantry and loved the joys of witty conversation. In her letters she confessed to her taste for puns, witticisms, and jokes, and this must have allowed her to feel quite at ease with the group surrounding Mme de Rambouillet. Moreover, she realized that her ready wit enabled her to lead a conversation wherever she wished: "She has a superior intelligence that allows her to dominate others. Thus one can be sure that she is able to have people near her say what she wishes them to, although they, in turn, are convinced that they are speaking their own mind" (*Cyrus* X, 335).

She does not, however, seem to have taken unfair advantage with her intellectual superiority, and according to what we know of her life she was a simple and honest woman:

There is no other person in the world so generous and concerned with the well-being of others. Furthermore, she is extremely faithful in her friendships, and with her soul so tender and her heart so passionate, it is undoubtedly a supreme joy to be loved by Sapho. This is also because she is ingenious in finding new ways to please those she loves and in making them aware of her affection without appearing to do anything extraordinary. She never fails to let those she loves know that she loves them dearly. Another admirable trait is her inability to be envious, and the ability to give credit generously to others for their accomplishments. She has more pleasure in praising others than being praised herself. (*Cyrus*, X, 335–36)

Ménage confirms Mlle de Scudéry's intellectual gifts in a letter published as the preface to Sarasin's *Oeuvres*. He mentions "[t]he rare knowledge that you so eminently possess."[31] This, coming from such an eminent scholar "who knew Greek as well as any one in France," takes on extreme value. Ménage also extols the tenderness and loyalty of her friendships, and we clearly can see proof of this in her correspondence. She seems to have been devoid of jealousy, as is evident in an examination of her work. Mlle de Scudéry was usually flattering in her portraits of friends and acquaintances, and it was rare that she showed any severity toward anyone.

For us today, Mme de Rambouillet is perhaps best known as Cléomire, as she is depicted in volume VII of *Cyrus*. It is noteworthy that everyone agreed on the excellence of her nature, which, according to Victor Cousin, "disarmed even Tallemant himself," a not unremarkable accomplishment when we consider how much he enjoyed writing naughty things about everyone. Mlle de Scudéry, in her portrait of Mme de Rambouillet, sought not only to picture her personality, but also to describe the effect it had on others:

Cléomire is tall, well proportioned, and all the features of her face are admirable. The delicacy of her coloring is beyond description, the majesty of her bearing is worthy of admiration, and a certain something shines from her eyes that inspires respect in the soul of all those who gaze upon her. As for me, I admit to you that I have never been able to approach Cléomire without feeling a certain respectful apprehension that obliged me to be more aware of myself, and I felt this more in her presence than anywhere else. . . . Her physiognomy is the most beautiful and the most noble I have ever seen, and the tranquillity that is apparent on her visage clearly indicates that it comes from her soul. One sees that her passions are compliant to her good sense and, therefore, do not trouble her heart. (*Cyrus*, VII, 296–297)

Beautiful and serene, Mme de Rambouillet was also a remarkably cultured woman: "Cléomire's mind is not like those that are limited to what nature has given them, because she has carefully cultured hers, and I think that it can be said that there is little knowledge of value that she has not acquired" (*Cyrus*, VII, 298). Mme de Rambouillet, however, did not play the role of pedant and never spoke without carefully maintaining the "decorum of her sex." This extremely high opinion of Mme de Rambouillet did not diminish throughout the years, and Mlle de Scudéry, in her *Conversations*, still wrote glowingly of Arthénice and the *Chambre bleue*.

It was during the most glorious years of the Hôtel de Rambouillet that Mlle de Scudéry was received and appreciated. There she acquired her polish, her ideas, and the manners that she would never lose. It was also there that she began to build her literary reputation. Even if her name had not appeared on *Ibrahim ou L'Illustre Bassa* or *Les Femmes illustres*, it was generally admitted that she did participate in writing them.

In March or April of 1639 she took part in the dispute over *I Suppositi* that, according to Magendie "set the Hôtel on fire."[32] Voiture and Mlle de Rambouillet were shocked by the style of Ariosto's play, which was in the tradition of Plautus and Terence. Chapelain, seconded by Mlle Paulet and the de Scudérys, defended the comedy. Through this episode Mlle de Scudéry established a name for herself, and Balzac, who was the mediator in the dispute, recognized that Madeleine de Scudéry was the equal of her brother: "This woman, who writes so elegantly, and with such good sense, is certainly worthy of her brother, and she is, to my taste, an excellent person" (R. 144). In regard to Mlle de Scudéry's opinion of the play, it was unequivocal: "I find it extremely pleasing. . . . In it I see nothing objectionable, and with the little knowledge I possess I perceive only great beauty" (R. 146). Rathery, the editor of her correspondence, was more prudish and granted that there were some dubious lines in the prologue at which Mlle de Rambouillet could justifiably take offense. In his *Réponse à deux questions ou du caractère et de l'instruction de la comédie*, Balzac underlines the characteristics peculiar to comedy which clearly distinguish it from tragedy. He commented: "It [comedy] travels on foot, but never lets itself fall in the mud."[33] Without having elaborated on her conception of comedy, Mlle de Scudéry, with her first known skirmish in the literary world, found herself not on the side of the prudes, who were so easily shocked by some vulgarity, but rather with those who were instinctively charmed by this play.

Mlle de Scudéry was to leave the pleasant surroundings of Paris after only five years of happy association with the salons that meant so much to her. Through the intervention of Mme de Rambouillet, Georges de Scudéry, brilliant, but totally unable to manage his finances, was appointed governor at Notre-Dame-de-la-Garde, a fortress that dominates the city of Marseille.[34]

Mlle de Scudéry, who lived with her brother in Paris, followed him when he went to take possession of his post. We have a good idea of these years away from Paris because of the correspondence she maintained with her friends there, although, unfortunately, most of it has been lost.

## IV  *L'ennui de mon exil*

Before going to Marseille, the de Scudérys first traveled by carriage to Rouen for the purpose of arranging some family affairs. In September of 1644, Mlle de Scudéry, in a letter to Mlle Robineau, a "woman of great wit and a close friend,"—according to Somaise—gave a vivid and humorous account of this trip. The four horses pulling the coach were emaciated and each of a different color. "Their gait was so slow and regular that there are no cardinals in Rome going to council who move with more solemnity that we did during our trip to Rouen" (R. 149). Was the company pleasant, at least, so as to make the trip more bearable? This too is doubtful, as Mlle de Scudéry draws a rather piquant picture of the other passengers. One was a young student "coming from Bourges" where he had just received a law degree. He constantly swore by Cujas, of whom Mlle de Scudéry pretended ignorance, and she commented that:

I finally learned that this Cujas was an ancient doctor of jurisprudence, and the student cited him in regard to everything. If one spoke of war he said that he would rather be a disciple of Cujas than be a soldier; if one spoke of travel he assured us that Cujas was known everywhere; if one spoke of music he said that Cujas was more precise in his judgements than music was with its notes; if one spoke of food he swore that he would rather fast than not be able to read Cuja. (R 152)

As for Mlle de Scudéry, she swore that she never wished to hear of Cujas again!

Returning briefly to Paris, the de Scudérys were soon on the road again, and on the 27th of November Mlle de Scudéry wrote a letter to Mlle Paulet from Avignon. This time she related, as Mme de Sévigné did herself, at a later time, the dangers of crossing the Rhône. Twice they nearly came to disaster on the treacherous waters, and she wrote that she was "well resolved never to cross so annoying a river again" (R. 156). The voyage, however, did have some charm, particularly during her stop at Avignon. After having visited the tomb of Petrarch's Laura at the monastery of the Observantines, she was surprisingly offered a room for the night.[35] She was then able to walk through the monastery gardens filled with orange trees, and "only four steps from the building where the members of the Inquisition were staying" (R. 158). While showing Mlle de Scudéry Laura's tomb, one of the monks related the story of her life as well as that of Petrarch. He also showed her a box containing a medal with Laura's portrait, a sample of Petrarch's poetry, and some poetry by Francis I. Mlle de Scudéry was astonished that these worldly objects were kept in the same place as religious relics. She concluded that if the monks, so close to the Inquisitors, were allowed so much latitude, what liberties were allowed the women of the city?

She amused herself with a taunting description of these women: "Among the more than a thousand women I have seen in church, only three of them used handkerchiefs." This is an allusion to the custom of covering one's low-cut neckline when in church (see the reference in *Tartuffe*). She went on to say: "What was even more surprising is that despite the lack of handkerchiefs, I did not even see one bosom. The only conclusion I can draw from this is that it is not so much that women with bosoms are covering themselves, but rather that those without, as a means of mortification, are making absolutely certain that everyone sees they have none" (R. 155–59).

Mlle de Scudéry finally arrived in Marseille, and her exile began. She wrote many letters at this time, and even if we have only a part of them, they do give us a good idea of her thoughts. The corres-

pondence with her friends, above all that with Mlle Paulet, is filled
with details, and even speaks of "follies" that were heightened because of her "proximity to the Orient."

She first mentioned the custom in Marseille to visit the newly
arrived, who had to be available for these visits during the first three
or four days of their stay. It was then necessary to return these
visits, and when she added them up she realized that she had to see
eighty persons. An unexpected charm to these encounters was the
fact that the majority of these visitors did not speak French. This did
not unduly disturb Mlle de Scudéry as she found that she had a
hidden talent for understanding *Provençal* and she even signed one
of her letters in this manner: "*Siou vuestra serventa affettionada*"
(R. 176).

Among the numerous visitors, mostly women, was Mlle de
Diodée. She was extremely pedantic, and Mlle de Scudéry wrote
amusingly of her constant references to "Trismegistus, Zoroaster
and other similar personages" (R. 168). For the lack of better company, Mlle de Scudéry continued to see her often during the first
two years of her stay in Marseille until a disagreement put an end to
their relationship. She was not forgotten, and appears in *Cyrus* as
Philiste (III, 164) if we are to believe the *clé*. In any case, the
frequency of visits slowed down appreciably when her visitors returned to their favorite pastime, a card game called *la basècle*. This
did not disturb Mlle de Scudéry in the least, and she announced
that even if they did return she would receive them in such a way as
to discourage other visits. She summed up the sadness of her situation when she wrote: "I frankly admit that while I am not unintelli-
gent enough to accustom myself to those who are, I don't have the
mental strength to find fulfillment in myself alone" (R. 167). It is
quite evident that she missed the Hôtel de Rambouillet and her
friends very much and tried to find their company again in her
correspondence. In *Clélie* she has one of the characters explain that
letters should not be literary, but rather "a conversation between
two people . . . filled with news, and if there is no news one should
invent some" (IV, 1139).

Mlle de Scudéry applied this principle to her own letters, and
there is an example of an amusing incident that happened during
her stay in Marseille. She had heard that Monsieur de Grasse was
coming and she awaited his arrival impatiently. M. de Grasse was
none other than her friend and former member of the Hôtel de

Rambouillet, Godeau, who had become bishop of Grasse and therefore, according to the custom of the time, was referred to as M. de Grasse. When she was told that he had finally arrived and was in the dining room, she rushed to his table, knowing that he did not stand on ceremony, and, according to her own description, saw that M. de Grasse was wearing "high boots, a lavish waistcoat, a scarlet mantle, a silver sword, and a beautiful grey hat plumed with yellow feathers" (R. 187). She goes on to say in her letter: "Don't think, Mademoiselle, that I am inventing all of this, because I saw M. de Grasse exactly as I have described him." Of course it is evident that she was not describing her old friend, the bishop, but rather, to her own embarrassment, a nobleman whose name was indeed, M. de Grasse. After having had a good laugh over this case of mistaken identity, she purposely withheld the information from her brother so that he too could make the same mistake.

Mlle de Scudéry also included in her letters descriptions of the landscape which she later remembered in detail and included in her novels. She wrote enthusiastically of the mild climate, the beauty of the jasmines and the orange trees, and the fruit that was found all year round. She also made this admission: the winter in Marseille was more beautiful than the spring in Paris.

Nevertheless, her extreme joy in returning to Paris literally burst from the pages of a letter written in haste a few hours before her departure. This letter to Mlle Dumoulin thanked her for a portrait of Mlle Schurman, a German woman renowned in all Europe for her knowledge. She further commented that Marseille, despite its charm, was no longer what it once was when the Romans themselves came there to study Greek. Now Paris was the one place that was worthy of doing homage to the erudition of a Mlle Schurman, and it was only there that she, Mlle de Scudéry, could possibly live (R. 204).

The return trip to Paris does not seem to have been the most rapid, and the de Scudérys took advantage of this last occasion to visit certain places of interest. They experienced two adventures during their trip. First, Renaudot's *Gazette* announced their death in attempting to cross the Isère (R. 35). A prompt correction reassured their friends. Then, according to an account told by Fléchier, in Lyon they faced the possibility of imprisonment. They were not traveling in the grand manner, and stopped at an inn where they took a room that had very thin walls. In the room next to them there was a nobleman from Auvergne who could not help but hear the conversation they were having. They were discussing whether or not they would kill the prince, evidently one of the characters of the novel they were presently planning. The nobleman, quite excited, thought that they were plotting an assassination attempt on Louis XIV and called the police at once. The adventure came quickly to a conclusion once the police officers asked their names: "Having established that they were M. and Mlle de Scudéry, they realized that they were discussing *Cyrus* and *Ibrahim* rather than King Louis, and that they had no plan other than killing a prince who had been long since dead."[36] This amusing story proves at least two things. First, the collaboration of brother and sister is clearly established, and second, the fact that the police knew the de Scudéry name at once indicates just how celebrated it was.

## V  Paris: "The only place"

When M. de la Vergne, Mme de Lafayette's father, failed to obtain for her the post of governess to Mazarin's nieces, Mlle de Scudéry continued to live with her brother.[37] Between the years 1649 and 1653 the ten volumes of *Le Grand Cyrus*, published by Courbé, appeared and were immensely successful. Georges de Scudéry was elected in 1650 to replace the grammarian Vaugelas at the *Académie française*, and Mlle de Scudéry resumed the life she led before her departure for Marseille. She visited the salons, saw her friends, took part in the brilliant social life, and yet found the time to write. The question arises as to when she did have the time to write. The answer probably lies in what she wrote of Sapho: "One did not know how much time she spent in writing because she saw her friends quite regularly and one almost never saw her either reading or writing. She had the time, however, to do whatever she wished, and her hours were so well organized that she had enough leisure time both for her friends as well as for herself" (*Cyrus*, X, 337). This was undoubtedly Mlle de Scudéry's secret: her schedule was so well organized that she found time to do everything she enjoyed, writing included. Her work also did not seem to reduce her social life, which was extremely active.

In 1649–1650 she took part in the great dispute between the supporters of Voiture, recently dead, and those favoring Benserade, who was trying to succeed him as the most fashionable poet of the time. The dispute was over Voiture's *Sonnet d'Uranie* and Benserade's *Sonnet de Job*. At that time the world of the salons was divided into two factions, each with definite political undertones. Rallying behind the Prince of Conti were the *Jobelins*, namely Conrart, Segrais, Scarron, and Princess Palatine. They all were admirers of Benserade's sonnet, whereas the faction favoring Voiture's sonnet was led by Mme de Longueville, and included Montausier, Sarasin, Desmarets, Mme Saintot, and Mlle de Scudéry. Balzac, at the request of Montausier, gave a fourteen page opinion and declared that: "In applying Aristotelian principles the two sonnets cannot be compared."[38] As a matter of fact, few could remain noncommittal in this literary battle, but Corneille and Mme de la Suze felt that the dispute was futile when compared to the actual civil strife that was tearing France apart.[39] Finally Halley, a professor of eloquence at Caen, exercizing great discretion, settled the dispute by declaring Voiture the winner.

Even if she had little admiration for the man himself, Mlle de Scudéry did take Voiture's part in the dispute, and clearly explained her reasons in a letter to Chapelain, dated December 7, 1649. She felt that although the last two lines of the sonnet of Job were delicate and beautiful, one had to read all of the other lines in order to get there. Furthermore, Job, for her, had an unpleasant and unclean association, and the proof of this is that no great painter, such as Raphael, Titian, or Poussin, was inspired to use him as a subject of a painting (R. 209).

Her letters of the time were also filled with details concerning the *Fronde*. Her position seemed ambiguous, and lent itself to confusion. Because of her loyalty to Mme de Longueville and to Condé she has wrongly been thought of as a *Frondeuse*. In a letter to Godeau, Mlle de Scudéry informed him that Mme de Longueville was in flight and that Condé was in prison. She further stated: "It is impossible to be untouched by their misfortunes" (R. 212). At the same time she detested their temporary allies, the Duc de Beaufort in particular, whom Parisians referred to as "The King of the Market" (*Le roi des Halles*). In November of 1650 she wrote that the Duc de Beaufort was badly received by the queen: "In leaving he encountered Cardinal Mazarin on the stairway. They greeted each other like people afraid of catching a cold, because instead of lifting their hats they pulled them even more tightly on their heads" (R. 234).

Once the rebellious princes were released, Mlle de Scudéry

turned her attention from them and concentrated more on her king, to whom she was always loyal. Her remarks in regard to him demonstrate a profound knowledge of psychology. In a letter of March 2, 1651, she reported that the young king, practically a prisoner in his palace, which was surrounded day and night by the *Bourgeois*, danced in a ballet by Benserade. She commented: "This makes me think of the little birds that rejoice in their singing although they are prisoners in their cages." Later in the letter she makes a prediction that eventually comes true: "The king seems to hate those who want to lessen his authority, and, judging from appearances, he will remember tomorrow what they are doing today" (R. 245). In fact, although his reign was a lengthy one, Louis XIV never forgot the difficulties of the *Fronde* and built Versailles in order to get away from the Parisians.

Despite her sympathy for the Condé family during the *Fronde*, Mlle de Scudéry was not criticized for it. Her brother, however, angered Mazarin, who returned after the conflict to an even more powerful position. Georges de Scudéry, knowing that he would be arrested, fled to Granville, near Le Hâvre, and this put an end to the living arrangements of the brother and sister.

It was at this time that Georges de Scudéry, fifty-three years of age, married a girl of twenty-seven, Marie-Madeleine de Montcal de Martinvast. She was greatly enthusiastic about novels and collaborated with her husband in the writing of *Almahide ou L'Esclave-reine*, in which Mlle de Scudéry had no part.[40] Mme de Scudéry was a witty woman, and after the death of her husband her salon was quite popular with the *Précieuses*, for whom she was known as Saraide.[41] She has left an extensive correspondence with Bussy-Rabutin, which is often mistakenly attributed to Mlle de Scudéry.

Around 1660 Georges de Scudéry was once again in the king's favor and returned to live in Paris. It seems that he wanted to resume living with his sister, but, according to Tallemant, she did not agree to it. Her reasons for this are not known, and one can only conjecture, but it is probable that Mlle de Scudéry, once having known the delight of being free to do as she wished, did not care to renounce this pleasurable way of life. From this point on there is no mention of Georges de Scudéry in any of her correspondence, and he seems to have vanished from her life. Whereas numerous letters express the profound grief she felt at the loss of friends such as Mlle Paulet, Pellisson, or Abbé Boisot, there is literally no mention whatsoever of any reaction to her brother's death in what remains of her correspondence. Ménage, however, reported that he wanted to know the date of Georges de Scudéry's death and requested this information of his sister. She replied with the date only and made no comment.[42] The assertion made in Georges de Scudéry's biography that "when he died on May 14, 1667, his sister felt the deepest sorrow of her life" seems, at the very least, to be an exaggeration.[43]

## VI  *The* Samedi *(Saturday)*

The name of Mlle de Scudéry is almost automatically associated with the *Samedi*, the day she chose to receive her friends at her house in rue de Beauce. The residence was situated in the Marais,[44] the most elegant section of Paris at the time. Although the house had some defects, it was still quite comfortable, and its beautiful garden was a source of inspiration for many poems. Being on the outer edge of the Marais, Mlle de Scudéry could enjoy the semirural surroundings of this still undeveloped area. A stereotyped picture of the *Samedi* has evolved as a meeting place for old maids and middle-aged gentlemen, poetizing in either a ridiculous or a pedantic manner. The viewpoint held by many critics is that Mlle de Scudéry's salon was attempting to replace the Hôtel de Rambouillet, of which it was only a ridiculous reflection.

First of all, this dichotomy of characterizing the Hôtel de Rambouillet as the symbol of elegance during the first half of the century, and then picturing the *Samedi* as a reflection of bad taste and ridicule in the years following the *Fronde*, is not supported by the facts. This comparison is an easy one to make, and it is found often in studies of the seventeenth century. But it is one that neither the dates nor contemporary literature justify. Gustave Charlier's remarkable article "La Fin de l'Hôtel de Rambouillet"[45] has clearly established that the activities of the Hôtel de Rambouillet continued until well after the *Fronde*. That the *Fronde* and family grief lessened, or even temporarily stopped, the meetings at the Hôtel de Rambouillet is understandable, but it did not put an end to Mme de Rambouillet's social life, and she did not die until 1665. Loret, in *La Muse historique*, chronicled Parisian life in verse, and mentioned that on July 17, 1662, the young *dauphin* was taken to visit the Hôtel de Rambouillet, which was "usually attended by people very carefully selected."[46]

One of the main criticisms of the *Samedi* is that it was supposedly frequented by the bourgeois, understood in the twentieth century to mean a group of middle class or mediocre persons. As Emile Magne has reminded us in *Le Salon de Mlle de Scudéry*,[47] the bourgeois of that time did, in fact, represent the élite of the seventeenth century. They frequented the *Samedi*, as well as the Hôtel de Rambouillet, or, for that matter, any of the elegant salons of the period.

The importance accorded the Hôtel de Rambouillet and, afterwards, the *Samedi*, mistakenly overshadows the fact that there were many other salons attended by more or less the same people. Adam tells us that Mme du Plessis-Guénégaud received at the Hôtel de Nevers, and that Mme Fouquet, Mme du Plessis-Bellière, and Mme Tallemant also had their salons. Emile Colombey, citing Somaize's *Dictionnaire des Précieuses*, counted no fewer than eighteen salons, and this did not even include the highly frequented and celebrated salon of Mme de Sablé.[48] The *Samedi* meetings were but one of many such gatherings in a milieu teeming with social activities where the nobility and rich bourgeois sought to fill their idle hours.

As for the activities of the *Samedi*, they were not greatly different from those of other meetings. This is not surprising when one considers that the same persons were attending more or less most of the various salons. For example, "Mme de Sablé left her own salon, a model of urbanity, to visit the *Samedi*, and Mme de Rohan-Montbazon also came in order to enjoy the charm of a conversation with Pellisson. Mme de Sévigné. was frequently a guest because she greatly admired Mlle de Scudéry."[49] According to M. Mongrédien,[50] one must also include as habitués of the *Samedi* Mme de Platbuisson, the abbess of Malnoue, Mme de Plessis-Bellière, Mme du Plessis-Guénégaud, Mme de Lafayette, Mme Scarron, Mme de Montausier; and we know, through *La Gazette de Tendre*, that the Duchess de Saint-Simon must also be counted among Mlle de Scudéry's illustrious visitors.[51] We see, then, that the *Samedi* was not a closed, middle class group that met exclusively at Mlle de Scudéry's salon, or at the salons of Mlle Boquet or Mme Aragonais, where the *Samedi* were sometimes held, but was a rather mobile group whose members were readily accepted in salons frequented by others not necessarily associated with the *Samedi*.

If the *Samedi* had a literary reputation, it was due to Mlle de Scudéry's personality and the presence of Conrart and Pellisson. This is not to say that it was an imitation of the *Académie française*.

It must be remembered that the main purpose of the salon was for amusement. Among the activities were excursions, elegant dinners, and surprise visits to friends staying in the country. The glory of a certain pastry shop in rue Saint-Honoré that Mlle de Scudéry and her friends loved to frequent has come down to us[52] and we also know of Mme Aragonais' dolls, which the ladies of the *Samedi* dressed in the current mode. Other diversions were the experiments done by Claude Perrault, architect and anatomist, to observe the chameleon's ability to change color according to its environment. These chameleons had been sent from Egypt as a present to Mlle de Scudéry, and the guests of the *Samedi* were delighted with this scientific experiment (R. 113–14).

Poems were exchanged, of course, as were certain gallantries, but all this was a part of the elegant way of life of the salon. Despite the delight that Pellisson and Conrart had in collecting and filing away the papers and letters that circulated at the *Samedi*, it does not seem that they did so with the intention of saving them for posterity. Louis Belmont, who published extracts from the *Chronique du Samedi*, cited Pellisson's original chronicle in which Sapho expressed her concern that the documents not fall into "profane hands," thus bringing ridicule on the salon by those who could not possibly comprehend its manners. At this point it should also be remembered that the idea of chronicling a salon's events did not originate with the *Samedi*. Emile Magne has pointed out that *La Gazette de plusieurs endroits* of the Hôtel de Rambouillet served as a model for all of the other gazettes to follow.[53]

One day, the 20th of December 1653, stands out particularly in the history of the *Samedi*. It has been called the *Journée de Madrigaux* because of the incredible number of madrigals, or short poems, written on that day. The account taken from the *Chronique du Samedi* demonstrates that, contrary to common belief, the guests of the salon did not take themselves seriously and were always aware that they were playing games: "A squire with literary aspirations was smitten by the latest craze and, with not a little effort, managed to compose a sonnet of *bouts-rimés*. The head footman wrote, at the very least, six dozen comic poems. But our heroes and heroines did nothing but write madrigals. . . . All was done gaily and without grimaces. No one bit his fingernails, and no one stopped laughing or speaking. All that was heard were challenges and answers, assaults and the return sallies."[54]

Sarasin, visiting Paris for what would be the last time, took part in the day of the madrigals, and, under the name of Polyandre, won the contest by writing eleven of them. During the visit he also wrote *Dulot vaincu ou la défaite des bouts-rimés,* which he entrusted to his friends before leaving to rejoin Conti, in whose service he found himself at the time. Death prevented him from putting the finishing touches on his work, but, according to Paul Festugière, it was "the first to date, and one of only two *poèmes héroi-comiques* that exist in French literature." He felt that Sarasin's work had a great deal of verve and was superior to that of Boileau's *Le Lutrin.*[55]

Pellisson and Ménage gathered Sarasin's works together and published them in 1656. For this Ménage wrote a dedication to Mlle de Scudéry, Pellisson wrote the preface, and Conrart signed the *privilège.* This work, then, can justly appear to be a "Manifesto of the Précieux" as has been suggested by Marcou.[56] Even if all the members of the *Samedi* were not of the same caliber as Sarasin, they certainly basked in the glory of his poetry.

Isarn, called Trasile by the members of the *Samedi,* was another poet of great charm, as is demonstrated by this *poème monorime* inspired by the *Samedi.*

> Que bénis soient les *Samedis*
> Que chaque semaine en ait dix,
> Que les Dimanches et Lundis
> Avec leurs seigneurs les Mardis
> Mercredis, Jeudis, Vendredis,
> Soient renvoyés au temps jadis
> Et que tous nos ans soient ourdis
> De vos aimables *Samedis.*[57]

> (Blessed be the *Samedis*
> If each week filled with ten could be,
> I'd send the Sundays and Mondays, you see,
> Along with Tuesdays, Wednesdays, and Thursdays, with glee,
> With Fridays to times gone by so happily,
> So that all our years could be
> Made up only of your lovely *Samedis.*)

He was also a seductive, handsome, and fickle young man. Sapho, the queen of the imaginary kingdom of *Tendre,* gave Isarn permission to leave her realm to enter the kingdom of "Dangerous Waters and Unknown Lands," a realm of passion that he visited often with great success. His lively interest in brief love affairs did not, how-

ever, prevent him from enjoying a highly valued platonic relationship with Mlle de Scudéry, for whom he admitted feeling "an ear-
nest and ardent affection and the most perfect friendship that one
had ever spoken of."[58]

Mlle de Scudéry did indeed possess intellectual and artistic qualities that her literary friends could not help but appreciate. These
qualities were very much in evidence during still another dispute
that aroused the world of the salons in 1656. Tallemant wrote an
account of the success that young Raincy had with a poem he had
written. He was very pleased with it, as was the *Samedi*. However,
Ménage, more or less jealous of Raincy's success, declared that the
poem had been translated from the Italian and had been written
by Tasso. He then produced this so-called poetry of Tasso, which,
of course, he himself had written. Raincy swore that his poem
was original, and his indignation was even greater when Ménage
added insult to injury by pointing out that Tasso's poem had already
been imitated in a poem by Guarini.

Mme de Sévigné, writing from Les Rochers, declared that the
Guarini appeared superior to the Tasso, but that the Raincy was also
admirable. Mme de Lafayette, writing from her castle L'Espinasse,
admitted her incompetence, but also admitted her preference for
the fake Tasso. Chapelain, the Chevalier de Méré, Costar, and
almost all of the *Samedi* favored "Tasso," and Mme de Rambouillet,
along with Mme de Sévigné, voiced her preference for the Guarini
poem. Only Mlle de Scudéry suspected the trickery, and she had
Ménage confess that he had put Raincy's poetry into Italian and that
Tasso had nothing to do with the affair.[59]

There was another dispute that caused a much deeper division
among the guests of the *Samedi*, and that was the matter of Gilles
Boileau's election to the *Académie française*. Ménage and Pellisson
opposed Boileau and drew Mlle de Scudéry to their side. Chapelain, on the contrary, supported Boileau, and this precipitated a
dispute of an importance that is difficult to understand today. The
explanation, according to Adam, was the fact that Gilles Boileau had
introduced to the literary disputes of the time a violence and malice
theretofore unknown. Pellisson failed in his attempt to block
Boileau's admission and did not attend any of the academy's meetings until Boileau's death.[60]

The guests of the *Samedi* were not only impassioned by discussions of a literary type. Many of their conversations pertained to a

detailed analysis of love. Naturally it was a question of noncarnal love, but this is perfectly understandable when one considers that in the seventeenth century marriage was largely a family matter in which love generally played no part. It therefore was especially difficult for many women, who often found themselves in a position where they neither loved nor even respected their husbands. As a result, some of them indulged in numerous love affairs, of which Tallemant, to give an example, has left us many interesting accounts. But others chose to forget the realities of life and transformed love into something intellectual. This was not necessarily done, however, only by unhappily married women. For many women, and men too, married or not, love was an intellectual occupation that inspired poems, gallantries, and conversations that helped them to fill the sentimental void in their lives.

It is this sort of intellectual love that is described in the *Carte de Tendre*, the most famous passage in *Clélie*. Of the thousands of pages that make up the novel, only a dozen are devoted to the map of this imaginary "country," which represents the paths that lead to the three kinds of spiritual love, and Mlle de Scudéry correctly feared that they might be badly interpreted. In the novel she has Clélie make this statement: "It is a momentary folly that I look on as nothing more than a trifle. For those who have the necessary wit to understand, it can be enjoyed merely as a novelty and a bit of gallantry" (I, 408–409).

It is important to note in regard to the *Carte de Tendre* that Clélie composed it for Herminius and not for Aronce, the man she fell in love with and eventually married at the end of the novel. Therefore, it is clear that the *Carte de Tendre* dealt with feelings of tenderness and had nothing to do with passion. It was concerned with an area of affection that particularly pleased poets and *Précieuses*. It mapped out the various stages of spiritual love, and although it was enthusiastically received in the salons, no one ever forgot that it was, after all, only a pleasant game.

In the novel the characters Clélie and Aronce, on the one hand, and Herminius and Valérie, on the other, went beyond the city of *Tendre sur Inclination* and eventually crossed the "dangerous sea" to the "unknown lands," the territory of physical love and marriage. As far as we know, Mlle de Scudéry herself chose not to visit these potentially threatening places.

According to the *Chronique du Samedi*, Mlle de Scudéry played the role of queen in this imaginary kingdom of Tendre and was also known as the *"Princesse d'Estime, Dame de Reconnaissance, Inclination et Terres adjacentes."* It was a game played by people in their forties or more, and that it had a childish aspect cannot be denied. However, it was in keeping with the taste of the time, and the *Samedi* was but one of the salons in which similar games were played. It should also be remembered that despite a certain frivolity that tends to evoke criticism today, the game did not lack in precision or acumen of a psychological nature.

## VII   *Paul Pellisson*

### A. *Acante and Sapho*

It was with Paul Pellisson that Mlle de Scudéry traveled to the land of *Tendre*. Paul Pellisson was extremely cultured and had the exceptional honor of being elected to the *Académie française* as a supernumerary. He studied law and was particularly interested in Latin culture. His biographer has said that he was never without his Horace.[61]

Mlle de Scudéry has given us a detailed description of his complex personality in two of her works. In *Cyrus* he is depicted as Phaon, and in *Clélie* he is seen as Herminius. She pointed out that in contrast to many flashy individuals who always seek admiration, Pellisson was very capable of remaining silent. However, when he wanted to speak he did so with brilliance. "As for his heart, it is grand, noble, tender, and generous. He is endowed with both integrity and goodness and is naturally liberal and just. In brief, Herminius has all the virtues and knows no vice. . . . He writes in both prose and poetry equally well and has composed serious and scholarly works that match the magnificence of their subjects. Others of his works are bantering and playful in tone and are filled with gallantry, accuracy, and all the spontaneity imaginable" (*Clélie* V, 156–57).

The duality of Pellisson's personality—great culture combined with gallantry—seems to have seduced Mlle de Scudéry, who quickly admitted him to the inner circle of the *Samedi*. Certain members felt that his entry was accomplished too quickly, and imposed a quarantine under the pretext that "on his way to Tendre he had passed through a place where there was a contagious disease."[62] This jealousy shown the newly arrived Pellisson finally subsided, and Mlle de Scudéry was able to declare him, in one of her most famous poems, "citizen of Tendre." She referred to him as Acante, his assumed name among the habitués of the *Samedi:*

> Enfin Acante, il faut se rendre
> Votre esprit a charmé le mien
> Je vous fais citoyen de Tendre,
> Mais, de grâce, n'en dites rien.[63]

> (At last Acante I must surrender,
> Your spirit has conquered my own,
> I pronounce you citizen of "Tender,"
> But I beg you let it stay unknown.)

The relationship that Mlle de Scudéry established with Pellisson was clearly spiritual, and it seems that it never went beyond that point. In *Cyrus* she described the love that united Sapho with her beloved Phaon: "There never were two hearts so united, and never did love join together so much innocence and so much ardor. They shared all of their thoughts, and did not even feel the need to express them aloud. They saw in each other's eyes what was in their hearts, and the tender feelings they saw caused them to love each other all the more" (*Cyrus* X, 504).

Twenty years later, in *Mathilde*, she described the bond between Petrarch and Laura, and it is reminiscent of the relationship between Sapho and Phaon. "Your rest will never be disturbed with matters that can divide you or with the domestic difficulties that disrupt the tranquility of married people. You have, if one is allowed to speak in such a way, all the flowers of love and friendship, and none of the thorns" (p. 41).

These are most likely among the reasons why Mlle de Scudéry and Pellisson chose to remain at *Tendre* and not run the risks of the *Mer dangereuse*. Another factor, perhaps less important, was the difference in their ages. In 1654 Sapho was in her forties, and Pellisson was seventeen years her junior. Neither one of them was physically attractive, and in a letter that Mme de Sévigné wrote to Mme de Grignan, she reported that Guilleragues accused Pellisson "of abusing the privilege that men have to be homely."[64] As a matter of fact, some unmercifully frank satirical poems of the time asked the question which of the two friends was the homelier.

Nevertheless, the mockery that they would have had to face up to does not seem, in itself, reason enough to explain their behavior. Another reason might well have been the influence that Pellisson's mother had on him. He generally signed his name as Pellisson-Fontanier, adding his mother's maiden name. This demonstrates the great respect he had for her. It is not difficult to imagine that Mme Pellisson's jealousy of Mlle de Scudéry had a definite effect on the relationship between Sapho and Acante. In any case, this is the impression we receive from Mlle de Scudéry's letters, and it certainly can explain why a marriage between the two was impossible. The most valid reason, however, for Mlle de Scudéry's celibacy probably lay in her well-known aversion to anything that could rob her of her freedom. She clearly expressed in *Cyrus* her fear of the husband that could become a tyrant: "I know quite well that there are many decent men, but when I think of them as husbands I also think of them as masters, and since masters have a tendency to become tyrants, I can, from that moment, only hate them. I then thank God for having given me a strong propensity against marriage" (*Cyrus*, X, 344).

In a letter of December 1691, written to Abbé Boisot upon the marriage of one of her friends, she commented on the opportunities she herself had to marry: "Three times in my life I have chosen freedom over wealth, and I have never regretted it" (R. 330). She admitted, however, that what was worthwhile for one person was not necessarily good for another, and that not all women loved their freedom as much as she.

It is this inclination toward independence that probably explains her attitude. She lived with her brother for a long time, and, if we believe Tallemant, he not only often prevented her from going out or receiving certain visits, he also placed obstacles in the way of her relationship with Pellisson. Once having been freed from this tyranny, we have no evidence, despite her unquestionable affection for Acante, that she ever wished to marry. She considered marriage to be a difficult undertaking to succeed in, and since Pellisson was known to be both touchy and stubborn, this did not encourage her to attempt such an adventure. A very strong affection seems, then, to be the extent of their relationship, but it was an extremely close one and not to be mistaken for the type of love that served as a distraction and little else. When they were separated they wrote each other every day, and this continued until Pellisson's death, some forty years later.[65]

## B. *The Closing of the Samedi*

Strangely enough, it was this very closeness that most likely led to the end of the *Samedi* rather than the state of ridicule into which it is reputed to have fallen. There is a fairly well-established theory that associates the demise of Mlle de Scudéry's salon with the lessening of her popularity as a writer. Both the *Samedi* and Mlle de Scudéry's novels supposedly disappeared after the success of the *Précieuses ridicules* in 1659. One can doubt the validity of this theory. First of all, Mlle de Scudéry's success as a novelist was far from over. *Clélie* reflected the spirit of the *Samedi,* and the success of the novel, first published in the years 1654 to 1660, was such that Courbé released a third edition from 1658 to 1662. This is to say that the first volumes of the third edition were being printed before the last volumes of the novel had even been written. This shows the continued infatuation the public had for the novel, and it certainly does not indicate that the author was ridiculed to the point of having to close her salon.

It is a fact, however, that the *Samedi* did come to an end sometime around 1659. A note from Pellisson to Mlle Bocquet asked: "Will it die, will it not die, our poor, our dear, our lovely Samedi?"[66] According to Belmont, the dispute that arose over Gilles Boileau's election to the *Académie française* played a role in the closing down of the *Samedi.* While this is not to be excluded, a more probable reason is the close alliance that Pellisson formed with Nicolas Fouquet, the minister of finance. Fouquet's biographer tells us that "Mlle de Scudéry and Pellisson were inseparable. To protect one meant to help the other as well."[67] Pellisson found himself growing more closely tied to Fouquet, described in *Clélie* under the name of Cléonime (X, 1088–89). The two men were alike in many ways. In both of them there was a mixture of a sense of seriousness, a knowledge of law and finance, and a love for poetry and gallantry.

Pellisson served Fouquet in two separate functions. One was as business secretary, and this meant working with him in affairs of finance and politics. At the same time Pellisson also served as protector of the literary world. He established a court for Fouquet, and acted as intermediary between the patron and the artists to be received and subsidized. The list of artists was long and it included many renowned authors such as the Corneilles, Scarron, and La

Fontaine. Pellisson had, according to Chatelain, in effect created "a kind of secretariat for the arts and sciences." Chatelain has also noted that all of Mlle de Scudéry's friends met at either Mme Fouquet's Parisian salon, at the castle of Vaux, or at their other property in Saint-Mandé.

They also met at the house of Fouquet's friend, Mme du Plessis-Bellière. She was depicted as Mélinthe in *Clélie*, and her house at Charenton was also well described in the novel (X, 879). The death of her parrot in 1654 provoked an avalanche of poems, and it was at this time the Fouquet launched the game of the *bouts-rimés*. This, in turn, inspired Sarasin to attack this fashionable pastime with his *poème héroi-comique, Dulot ou La Défaite des bouts-rimés*. It seems quite evident that this ambiance must have been quite familiar to the guests of the *Samedi*, and they could not help but feel perfectly at ease in such a milieu. As a matter of fact, the *Samedi's Royaume de Tendre* was quite similar to Fouquet's *Royaume Incarnadin*. Both mythical kingdoms had their topography, their assumed names, their colors, and their rules of gallantry. Fouquet loved riddles and the poetry of the *Précieuses*, and he himself wrote poetry that has survived to the present time. To pass, therefore, from *Tendre* to the *Royaume Incarnadin* was not difficult for the guests of the *Samedi*, and it seems that it became necessary due to Pellisson's close involvement with Fouquet. The *Samedi* might well have appeared to be a waste of time, since the activities at Fouquet's salon were comparable and took place in a setting infinitely more pleasant and luxurious. Isn't this reason enough, then, to conclude that Sapho let "the poor, the dear, the lovely *Samedi*" come to an end rather than to assume that it was done because of ridicule, for which there is no proof?

The closeness of the relationship between Fouquet and the guests of the *Samedi* also tends to refute the theory that it was Sapho and her friends who were satirized in Molière's *Les Précieuses ridicules*. Adam has suggested in "La Genèse des *Précieuses ridicules*" that Fouquet invited Molière to Vaux, and in doing so encouraged him to lighten his attacks on the *Précieuses*.[68] First of all, Fouquet himself was a *Précieux* during his youth, during the height of his career, and even during the years he spent in prison, where he continued to compose poems and poetic riddles.[69] Since this is the case, could he have invited Molière to Vaux in 1660, some months after the presentation of *Les Précieuses ridicules*, if he had felt that it was an attack on *Préciosité?* Mme de Guénégaud, one of Mlle de Scudéry's friends, and portrayed in *Clélie* as Amalthée, invited Molière to present his play at her home.[70] This surely indicates that she, too, did not view the comedy as an attack on her friends.[71]

There is another factor, of a psychological order, that enters the picture. Pellisson does not seem to have been capable of forgiving an insult, as was clearly demonstrated by his refusal to return to the *Académie française* while he risked encountering Gilles Boileau. Considering his role in Fouquet's life, is it not logical to assume that he could have convinced him to do without the actor-playwright if he had felt that Molière had offended their friends and ridiculed their pastime?

Even admitting that Fouquet was desirous of following the mode that made Molière an attraction of value, was it necessary for Pellisson to write the prologue to Molière's *Les Fâcheux*, presented at Vaux in 1661? It is difficult to believe that Pellisson, a man who could be stubborn and quite firm in his convictions, could have forgiven Molière so soon if he believed that he had ridiculed his dearest friends. An action of this type would have been absolutely incompatible with what we know of the *opiniâtre* Acante. Despite certain precautions that Mlle de Scudéry took in portraying him in *Clélie*, we can clearly see this aspect of his character: "He has sometimes been reproached for being stubborn and somewhat quick-tempered, but as for myself I have scarcely seen signs of stubbornness that could not have been reasonably taken for steadfastness. One can also say that his stubbornness is well meant because it arises only when he believes that he is correct. As for his temper, it is true that if he did not restrain himself he could appear at times to be a little sensitive" (V. 156–57).

## C. *The Fall of Fouquet*

If Pellisson was obstinate in his disputes, he was equally resolute in his loyalties. When Fouquet lost favor with the court, was arrested, and put into prison in September of 1661, Pellisson underwent the same treatment. While in prison he lampooned Fouquet's enemies, and also wrote a superb discourse in his defense that Voltaire ranked with the works of Cicero.[72] This becomes all the more remarkable when one considers that Pellisson did this while in great danger himself and at a time when only three other authors—La Fontaine, Dehénault, and Mlle de Scudéry—wrote in Fouquet's behalf.[73] It is not that Fouquet lacked supporters, but rather that most were afraid to express themselves publicly. Mme de Sévigné, also very closely tied to Fouquet's salon, has described in her correspondence this frightening period when everyone feared that Fouquet, who had aroused the king's jealousy and anger, would be put to death.

At the time of Pellisson's arrest Mlle de Scudéry was without news from him for twelve days. This prompted a most beautiful letter that she addressed to Pellisson while still unaware that he had been arrested, and it clearly demonstrates the depth of their feelings for each other: "I want nothing but a word that tells me how you are, because as long as I know that you are alive I will assume that you still love me and that you think of me as much as I do of you" (R. 79–80).

At the beginning of his imprisonment Pellisson had certain privileges, but when it became obvious that he would not give any evidence against Fouquet, he was put into a dungeon where his life became almost intolerable. It was during the long months he spent in solitary confinement that he succeeded in taming a spider. Despite the inherent difficulties, he was able to smuggle letters out to Sapho, who burned over five hundred messages sent to her from Pellisson during his stay at the Bastille (R. vi). During this time Mlle de Scudéry sought to obtain an easement of Pellisson's imprisonment or his release. When he finally was able to have visitors, she spent the entire day with him, and together they received all of Paris in his prison cell.[74]

After Pellisson's release from prison in 1666, Fouquet remained in confinement until his death in 1680. In a letter to her daughter announcing Fouquet's death, Mme de Sévigné also described Mlle de Scudéry's grief over the loss of a friend to whom she remained loyal throughout the years.[75] Pellison's fate was much happier than Fouquet's inasmuch as he was able, after his release, to demonstrate his loyalty to the king and win his favor. He made what seems a sincere conversion to Catholicism, and became historiograph and secretary to the king. At the end of his life he was involved in distributing funds to each Protestant who converted to Catholicism. He worked extensively during this liberal period and had no part in the brutal treatment of Protestants that led to the revocation of the Edict of Nantes.[76]

Mlle de Scudéry, like Pellisson, enjoyed the king's favor. Louis XIV awarded her a handsome pension, and she went to court to thank him. In one of Mme de Sévigné's letters there is a description of this touching event: "She was received in utter perfection; it was an audience designed only to receive this marvelous Muse. The king spoke to her and before she could kneel to kiss his knees he lifted her to his embrace."[77]

## VIII   *A Glorious Old Age*

For several years there existed a romantic picture of an aging Corneille living in poverty. A similar picture of Mlle de Scudéry also exists in which she, too, lived to see her work held in contempt: "Mlle de Scudéry knew . . . the sorrow of growing old in a society that she could not understand and in which she was no longer understood or appreciated. She outlived her influence and her glory, and her last years were spent living in regret."[78]

This seems to be quite different from the actual situation. First of all, her novels had certainly not been forgotten, as is indicated by the fact that an English translation appeared in the years between 1653 and 1677, and a translation into Castilian came out in 1682. Furthermore, between 1680 and 1694 Mlle de Scudéry published conversations taken from her novels, which she herself edited and completed. These excerpts more closely corresponded to the current mode of the *Nouvelles* which supplanted the long novel, and they were quite successful.

Mlle de Scudéry's declining health materially limited her activities, and in 1690 Mme de Sévigné prematurely told of her imminent death.[79] However, despite rheumatism, the colds that lasted longer each winter, and the deafness that became so total that it was necessary for her to communicate in writing, she managed to lead an active life, and published her last book of *Conversations* at the age of eighty-five. In a letter written to Huet in 1692, she assured him that she was the same, except for her ears that are worth nothing (R. 353). In a previous letter to Huet she admitted visiting a healer that he had recommended, but it was to no avail.[80] It is known that in 1666 Mlle de Scudéry began to feel the effects of the deafness that would overwhelm her, and which led Cotin to write these rather unkind lines:

> Les écrits de Sapho menèrent tant de bruit
> Que cette nymphe en devint sourde. (R. 131)

"The writings of Sapho made so much clatter that it caused the nymph to grow deaf." Despite her handicap Mlle de Scudéry remained as active as in the past. Even if she traveled less, her letter writing made up for the visits she was no longer able to make. In her letters to Abbé Boisot she recounted everything that happened in Paris or in Europe, and we can appreciate the wide range of her information. In 1692 she told of an earthquake in Paris that "was so strong that all those who found themselves in Notre-Dame fled the church believing that it was going to tumble down." As for Mlle de Scudéry, her deafness protected her because she believed the muffled sound she heard to be "a cat locked in the closet who wanted to get out," and she wrote of being not in the least frightened. Added to this news was what Pellisson had written to her, what the lady delivering the milk had told her, and, as a postscript, what she had just heard from Versailles (R. 347–48).

Far from being abandoned and ignored, she received an abundant correspondence, and still led, despite her advanced age, a life that interested her immensely. In one of her letters she excused herself for not having been able to speak to someone who had visited her because at the time there were too many guests in the house (R. 349). In August 1694 she excused herself once again for not being able to answer one of her correspondents as, she wrote, "I was overwhelmed on my saint's day with flowers, fruit, and poetry" (R. 379). In a letter of October 1699 to Mme de Chandiot she included a little *impromptu* "which she could not restrain herself from writing." This at the age of more than ninety! (R. 388)

The only great pain of what was otherwise a serene old age was the death of her old friends, and mainly of Pellisson in February 1693. Although he was ill he had no idea that he was dying and did so without benefit of confession and the last rites. There were those who took advantage of the situation to accuse Pellisson of not having been sincere in his conversion to Catholicism, and Mlle de Scudéry, as she did when Pellisson was a prisoner in the Bastille, once again took up her pen to defend his reputation. She moved heaven and earth in appealing to all of their friends, and obtained Bossuet's help. He was a great admirer of Pellisson, and admitted to reading every year his poem *Eurymédon*,[81] written for Mlle de Scudéry while he was in the Bastille. Bossuet's intervention and a beautiful eulogy written by Fénelon, who replaced Pellisson at the *Académie française*, succeeded in silencing the gossipmongers.

The eulogy that Mlle de Sudéry sent to Abbé Boisot summed up all that Pellisson had meant to her: "The king has lost the most zealous of his subjects, the century one of its great ornaments, literature one of its brightest lights, and religion one of its great defenders. But I have lost much more than all the others because I have lost a wonderful friend of forty years, with whom I have shared both good and bad times and for whom I have always felt the greatest of admiration" (R. 354). In his daily letters Pellisson mentioned his bad state of health, but no one could have foreseen his death coming so suddenly. Mlle de Scudéry, utterly unprepared for such a blow, was stricken with grief, but the need to defend Pellisson's memory helped her to overcome the pain.

Little by little the ranks of her friends began to thin out. In April of 1701 she lamented in a letter to Huet the death of Segrais. "He was one of my friends for fifty years" (R. 391). In answering someone who had flattered her with the possibility of being immortal she replied in this way:

> Quand l'aveugle destin aurait fait une loi
> Pour me faire vivre sans cesse,
> J'y renoncerais par tendresse,
> Si mes amis n'étaient immortels comme moi. (R. 530)

Clearly she could not consider immortality if her friends could not share it with her. In another *impromptu*, she made this statement in regard to immortality: "I would give up my part of immortality for a century of life" (R. 530). she did not quite achieve this goal, but was close to it, dying in June of 1701 at the age of ninety-four. The morning of her death saw her arise and prepare herself as was her custom, but not being able to stay on her feet she understood that death was near. She made her confession and died kissing her crucifix.

This Christian death seems to be the logical result of an untroubled religious life. The seventeenth century was a time of bitter religious disputes, but Mlle de Scudéry did not take part in them, and does not appear to have suffered from religious anxiety. According to Bosquillon's eulogy[82] she had even composed some religious poems intended strictly for her use or for that of "her most illustrious friend." At a time and place in which even the least important of one's writings circulated widely among the various circles, this rare discretion on Mlle de Scudéry's part most assuredly demonstrates the depth of her religious feelings. There is no doubt that she had utter confidence in "that admirable Architect who created the world" (*Entretiens de morale*, I, 184).

Having lived a life filled with goodness, honesty, and loyalty, Mlle de Scudéry died in peace. Most likely she was convinced that she was about to rejoin her departed friends for an eternity of gallant conversation.

CHAPTER 2

# The Novels: "The Pleasant Liars or the Folly of the Wise"

SOMAIZE tried to make us believe that the *Précieuses* referred to novels in this way, but it is a terminology that Mlle de Scudéry, to be sure, never utilized. It reflects quite well, however, the ambiguous position of these books that were avidly read by a public generally ashamed of its interest in literature considered to be second-rate.

*Ibrahim, Cyrus,* and especially *Clélie,* which was "the best-selling book of the century"[1] were great favorites of seventeenth century readers. It does not seem, as is pointed out in Maurice Magendie's work *Le Roman français au XVIIème siècle de l'Astrée au Grand Cyrus,* that innovation was the cause of their popularity. As a matter of fact, the essential characteristics of this genre had already been utilized in previous works. To begin a novel *in medias res* had been traditional since the *Ethiopiques,* and it meant that the chronology would be so complex that even the *nouveau roman* with its labyrinthian technique of jumping around in time would seem rather straightforward. The main plot unfolds throughout different episodes, not always in a chronological order, and is interlaced with numerous subplots. This might well disturb us today, but it had a particular charm for the seventeenth century reader, as Scarron in his *Roman comique* has pointed out. The use of conversations dates back to *La Cyropédie,* Camus used the idea of the *parfaite amitié,* (which was quite close to Mlle de Scudéry's *tendre amitié*), and digressions played a large part in *L'Astrée.*[2]

The best explanation for the great success of these novels, signed by Georges de Scudéry, probably lies in the personality of his sister, their actual author. As a matter of fact, it has been well established by Tallemant and Bosquillon[3] that Mlle de Scudéry wrote these three bestsellers, even if some critics have been reluctant to credit her with *Ibrahim* and *Cyrus*. In fact, it is impossible today to ascertain exactly what part Georges de Scudéry played in the writing of these books. In any case, their success seems to have come as a result of their ability to correspond to the public's taste. Mlle de Scudéry was able to sense any change in literary taste, and could respond to it immediately rather than after the fact. During the period that Paul Bénichou refers to as the time of "morale héroique," Mlle de Scudéry wrote heroic novels; and when this became passé she turned to the *nouvelle* and wrote *Célinte*. At this same time her brother wrote *Almahide*, a novel in eight volumes, which had only one edition because the public had already begun to lose its taste for this genre. At the end of the century the volumes of *Conversations morales* expressed a "morale mondaine" that greatly interested the readers of that time.

## I   Ibrahim ou l'illustre Bassa

### A. *Preface*

*Ibrahim* is in four volumes and was published in 1641. Its most unusual preface[4] contains the rules that govern the composition of the heroic novel. The style is quite rigid, even arrogant at times, and it is tempting to think that if Georges de Scudéry did not write it, he probably had a hand in its editing. His liking for theoretical disputes is well known because of the *Querelle du Cid*, but it would be excessive to credit him with being the sole creator of this text, as it expresses the rules that Mlle de Scudéry has applied to all of her heroic novels.

The first point made in the preface is that works of art should not be produced haphazardly but should follow a certain number of rules. Then there is a declaration that expresses respect for the Ancients: "Since we cannot be knowledgeable except for what others teach us, and since those that come last must follow what has come before, I decided that in drawing up the plan for this work, it was necessary to consult the Greeks, who have been our first masters." There should be a main plot that begins *in medias res* and there will also be subplots. The principal action should begin and end within a period of one year, with previous events learned through narratives. The author can take certain liberties, as Virgil did, in regard to chronology, and can have his heroes live in a period that is not exactly theirs.

Despite this, however, he must not, in any case, go beyond the bounds of probability. The author should also choose an illustrious personage for his hero and should be acquainted with that character's epoch and country. This will allow him to impart a certain local color to the story, as is done in *Ibrahim*, where the descriptions and the vocabulary produce a well-researched effect. It is necessary, however, not to go too far in this. The use of extraordinary occurrences, such as shipwrecks to revitalize the plot of a novel, should be limited, and monsters should be banned.

The respect for plausibility also dictates that the various adventures be distributed among different characters. It is not wise to confront the hero with a situation that would overwhelm even Hercules: "In order to represent the heroic spirit it is undoubtedly necessary to have the hero do something extraordinary, as in a moment of heroic rapture, but this should not continue too long or it will degenerate into something ridiculous and will not have any good effect on the reader." This is a valuable principle, which is, unfortunately, not always applied in *Cyrus* and *Clélie*, where the heroines are abducted several times and always saved by the heroes. This does give a new start to the action but not without a certain monotony.

In regard to the hero, it is necessary to describe him vividly. The author should not be limited to describing the hero's deeds, but should also allow him to express himself: "I am not interested in external things or the caprices of destiny; I wish to know the impulses of his soul and the way they are expressed." The knowledge of the hero's internal motivations allows one to know and appreciate him better.

D'Urfé was a master of this type of study to the point that "one could call him a portraitist of the soul." This depiction of the passions that motivate the hero, mainly love and ambition, should have a moral foundation. The righteous will be rewarded at the end, and the evil ones punished unless they are able to obtain forgiveness from Heaven through sincere repentance. The novel, therefore, is a moral work. It should also follow the rules of propriety and not contain anything "that women could not read."

The preface also contains a study of what the style of a novel should be and gives us a precise description: "The more fluent it is, the more beautiful it becomes; it should flow like a stream and not seethe like a torrent. It becomes more perfect when it is less constrained. I have tried then to strike a happy medium between the highflown and the ignominious. I have kept myself in check in the narratives and have freed myself for passionate matters. I have tried to speak not extravagantly and not too commonly, but like the *honnêtes gens*."

The style of a novel, therefore, should harmonize with the taste of its readers. The novels, after all, were meant for them, and thanks to these scrupulously followed rules, they were able to maintain their popularity for several decades.

### B. *Historical Basis*

In *The Turk in French History, Thought and Literature*,[5] Clarence D. Rouillard has carefully analysed Mlle de Scudéry's sources and borrowed material, noting the seriousness of her research. She not only used traveler's accounts but also read Chalcondyles, from whom she obtained historical background, elements of decor, and some vocabulary. The basic story of Ibrahim was found in Giovio's *Histoires*, which she then fashioned to her own needs. This former Greek slave had become the favorite of the sultan, whom we know as Suleiman II. After a period of great favor, sustained by many military victories, he incurred the sultan's anger. Encouraged by his wife, who was jealous of Ibrahim's political influence, Suleiman put him to death. Mlle de Scudéry retains the general framework but transforms the Greek slave into a prince of the Palaeologus family, supposedly born in Genoa. This is in agreement with the rules laid down in the preface that require that heroes be of high rank.

Since a major portion of the story takes place in Constantinople, Mlle de Scudéry generously utilizes local color and Turkish words in her descriptions. For example, she defends her use of the word "seraglio," which has connotations that could be considered shocking: "The old seraglio was the one place in the Orient where there was the most virtue and the least vice. This is because it was occupied by the mother, the aunts, the daughters, and the sisters of the emperor, who had no connection whatsoever with the sultan's harem."[6]

The novel opens with a remarkably colorful description of a triumphant procession in the Hippodrome celebrating one of Suleiman's great victories. The procession includes soldiers with exotic names, animals such as elephants and camels, and prisoners dressed in unusual costumes, some adorned with brilliant jewels befitting their station. This description has been greatly admired. Mme de Genlis,[7] for example, found it to be quite striking and noted that this novel, which she considered to be Mlle de Scudéry's best work, has been the inspiration for several well-known plays. This admiration for *Ibrahim* has been shared by many critics, and it is noteworthy that it was still being printed as late as 1723.

## C. *The Main Plot*

In 1923 E. Seillière published an abridged edition entitled *Isabelle Grimaldi* which consisted only of the main plot. He made this comment in his preface: "In order to be able to appreciate, without too much effort, this charming and delicate work today, it is necessary beforehand to eliminate the overwhelming excesses that corresponded so well to seventeenth century tastes".[8] Strangely enough, a comparison between Seillière's text and that of the original demonstrates that the latter has much more charm, and we find ourselves in agreement with the seventeenth century reader. Stripped of its subplots, the novel has, in effect, a dryness that is not found in the original. To be perfectly honest, however, it must be said that *Isabelle Grimaldi* is easier to follow.

Despite the sultan's favor and the many battles he has won, "Ibrahim Bassa could not conquer the melancholy that surrounded him amid all of his victories and all of his honors. . . . Destiny had given him what he did not at all desire, and had taken away the only thing he ever longed for" (I, 44).[9] Suleiman notices Ibrahim's sadness and wishes to know its cause. Ibrahim tries to hide the truth from the sultan and says that his uneasiness comes from the insecurity of his position. If he loses favor, his life is in danger, and, despite his desire to do well, he is afraid to make mistakes. The sultan assures him of his favor and friendship, and as proof he offers him his daughter Astérie's hand in marriage, saying: "I swear by Allah that as long as Suleiman lives you shall not die"(I, 53).

Ibrahim does not wish to marry Astérie, and therefore must reveal to Suleiman the true reason for his sadness. He tells of his love for Isabelle, whom he knew in Genoa at the time he was free and known by his true name as Justinian. He states that he cannot live without her, and then tells Suleiman the "story of Justinian and Isabelle," which is reminiscent in some ways of Romeo and Juliet.

The two young people belong to feuding Genoese families. Justinian returns to Genoa after having taken part in the wars lead by Emperor Charles V. He is an accomplished young man, and Isabelle is the most beautiful girl in the city. One evening they meet at a concert, and Justinian changes color "twenty times in an instant." The young girl also experiences a bolt from the blue, and it seems that they both have fallen in love at first sight. Justinian later states that he "obtained the permission to love her provided that his actions and words did not arouse any suspicions concerning their feelings" (I, 74).

Isabelle conducts herself quite decisively and allows the young man to see her and speak to her as often as circumstances permit. Since she spends several days in the country, he manages to go too, and is able to steal into her room at night: "Our conversation was so long that the awakening of the birds told me that it was time to let her sleep." In order to reassure her readers of the innocence of these daring nocturnal visits, Mlle de Scudéry has Justinian add: "She allowed me to kiss her hand through the lattice upon leaving, and it was the only favor she bestowed upon me during all the nights that I spent with her" (I, 84).

The secret of their nightly encounters is discovered, however, and Rodolphe, Isabelle's father, seeks to have Justinian assassinated. The attempt fails, and the wounded Justinian comes to the aid of Rodolphe, who is himself attacked by political enemies. Confronted with the magnanimity of this young man who has just saved his life, and whose life he had tried to take, Rodolphe decides to forget the feud separating the two families and allows the young couple to marry. Rodolphe announces that upon his death they will inherit the principality of Monaco and reign together.

Before the wedding can take place, however, Justinian is banished because in saving Rodolphe's life he killed a young man from a very influential family. He returns to the army and there he learns of Rodolphe's death. He is also given the false information that Isabelle has been forced by her mother into a rich marriage. "Since the body and the mind are so closely linked that one cannot suffer without the other, I fell ill" (I, 114). Once his body is cured, if not his soul, he takes part in a naval battle in which he is taken prisoner, sold as a slave, and then sent to Constantinople. After a rebellion of slaves, Justinian is ordered to be executed. On the way to the execution he passes by Suleiman's daughter Astérie, who takes pity on the young man and is able to obtain a pardon for him.

Little by little Justinian gains the confidence of the sultan through his political ability, his courage in battle, and his culture. They pass many hours in discussing history, music, and art. Mlle de Scudéry is careful to point out that Suleiman knew the *"langue franque,"* a kind of corrupted Italian that was spoken in the Orient for commercial use, and since Justinian was a Genoese, he could understand it (I, 254). A problem now arises: the position of confidence that Justinian occupies should not be held by a Christian. He refuses, however, to convert to Islam, but is persuaded to compromise by taking a Turkish name and by wearing local apparel.

When Suleiman learns all of Justinian's past he has pity, but cannot free him because he now has too much need for his services. The Sultan grants him, however, a leave of absence of six months in which he can visit Isabelle, and obtains, through his ambassador, the revocation of the young man's banishment.

Justinian and Isabelle then have the great joy of seeing each other again after having believed that they were separated forever. Justinian relates all of the adventures that had befallen him, and Isabelle explains that thinking him to be dead she decided never to marry, and to spend the rest of her life governing the principality of Monaco. Her beauty attracts numerous suitors, whom she discourages, but two of them try to abduct her. Luckily she is able to thwart their attempts.

Their happiness, however, is bittersweet because of the knowledge that Justinian must soon return to Suleiman. Isabelle's conduct is heroic, and she makes no attempt to dissuade him from his duty: "Please know that my heart is big enough to not allow you to dishonor yourself in proving your love for me, and I am delighted that you have as much regard for self-respect as I" (II, 224). She then suggests that they marry and both go to Constantinople. Justinian, knowing the inflammable nature of the sultan, and fearing that he might be too susceptible to Isabelle's charms, refuses. He foresees insurmountable complications ahead and therefore leaves Monaco without Isabelle to return to his life as Ibrahim the Bassa. Before departing he leaves this note: "I am leaving then, Madame, or perhaps it is better to say that I am being separated from myself in being separated from you" (II, 279).

When he arrives in Constantinople he learns that Suleiman has lost half of his kingdom because of having placed too much confidence in Sultana Roxelane's political ability. Ibrahim is able to correct the situation and recover the lost territories, but "he becomes the unhappiest of men" (III, 274). Doctors are consulted but they can do nothing because the source of Ibrahim's sickness is in his soul. Roxelane then suggests that they abduct Isabelle, and this is accomplished by Rustan, the sultana's henchman. When the young girl arrives in Constantinople "those who see Ibrahim have no doubt that Suleiman has found the exact remedy needed to rid him entirely of his melancholy. His eyes are brighter, his color higher, his speech stronger, and his gait more steady" (III, 320). Unfortunately, however, Ibrahim had been correct in his earlier fears, and the moment Suleiman lays eyes on Isabelle he begins to feel an uncontrollable emotion rising in him. He tries to fight it, but while the Bassa is away at war Suleiman declares his love to Isabelle, and it seems that his passion for her has overcome his feeling of friendship for Ibrahim.

When Ibrahim returns, victorious as usual, Isabelle tells him what has happened, and they both decide to flee. They plan to leave in the company of some Christians, also prisoners in Constantinople, whose stories provide the subject for many of the subplots. Unfortunately their plan is discovered, and they are caught at sea just when they believe that they have succeeded in their flight for freedom.

When they are once again in Constantinople, Suleiman sends Ibrahim a black robe, which means that he must die. Shortly before the time of the execution the sultan remembers the promise he once made that Ibrahim would never die while he, Suleiman, was still alive. Nevertheless, he still wishes to rid himself of the Bassa, and Roxelane, who wants to oblige him, consults a mufti for advice on how to eliminate the young man without violating the sultan's promise. The mufti suggests that since sleep is a kind of death, Ibrahim could be killed during Suleiman's slumber and the promise would remain inviolate. The sultan then retires, and Rustan waits for him to fall asleep so that he can give the order for the mute to kill Ibrahim.

Suleiman's conscience, however, will not let him sleep, and Mlle de Scudéry comments that "he was angry not to be able to be master of his own mind" (IV, 375). This scene constitutes one of the novel's most attractive moments. Several times Rustan moves toward the door believing the sultan to be asleep only to be quickly stopped each time. Suleiman then begins to reflect on his difficulty in falling asleep, and comes to the conclusion that it is a sign that Heaven is protecting Ibrahim. He realizes that his acts are criminal and that Ibrahim is innocent. "Repentance, which was an unknown feeling to me, is now ridding my heart of its love for Isabelle, and this love is being replaced with my feeling of friendship for Ibrahim. I feel it happening. Reason is taking its place again in my heart" (IV, 387).

He decides to grant the two lovers, as well as their friends, their freedom. Finding it impossible, however, to divulge the truth to everyone, he decides to disguise Ibrahim's departure by announcing his death to the populace. The people of Constantinople are so enraged by this that they lynch Rustan. In regard to this denouement, which is historically incorrect, Mlle de Scudéry makes this tongue-in-cheek comment: "The feigned death of Ibrahim was carried out so well that everyone believed it. In fact, it has led Giovio, and all the others who have written about Suleiman's reign, to the conclusion that the grand vizier Ibrahim did, indeed, die in this fashion. But in reality, the affair happened as I have described it" (IV, 394). Justinian and Isabelle return to Monaco where they marry and reign happily ever after.

## D. *The Subplots*

There are two groups of subplots. One involves the Christians, who are either French or Italian, and the other is dedicated to the Persians or the Turks. These stories are complicated, but each one is interesting in its own right.

The most fascinating one of all is unquestionably the story of the French marquis, whose pleasant personality will be found again in the character of Amilcar in *Clélie*. His adventures are related in three different stories. In the first we make his acquaintance and learn the reasons for his exile. He was accused of having deserted at the battle of Pavia, which is absolutely not true. He wanted the retraction of this false charge written in his accuser's blood, but François I, who knew the truth, took it upon himself to speak in defense of the marquis' honor. The king thought that this would be sufficient, but the marquis insisted that he wished to settle the affair himself, with épée in hand. This displeased the king, and the marquis, realizing that he had offended his sovereign, decided that it would be best to exile himself (II, 6).

Thus, he travels to Genoa where he meets other personages in the novel, with whom he will be taken to Constantinople. The quality that all of the adventures in the world could not take away from the marquis is his good humor. He is always in love, but never with the same woman, and the only thing that frightens him is marriage.

In a long speech that is half serious, half bantering, he describes the essence of *galanterie,* being quite careful not to encroach upon the rights of husbands:

There are no husbands who take pleasure in wearing a bracelet of their wife's hair, who ask of them only little favors, who are delighted to kiss just the tip of their gloved hands, or to say gallant things to them, to praise their beauty, to serenade them, to compose poems to their glory, and to say that they die of love for them. Does it not seem strange that these husbands, who do not love, and yet completely possess their women, would deprive us, who truly love them, of the little things that in no way compromise their virtue? (II, 40–41)

Despite the rational tone of this argument, it has no effect whatsoever on the husbands, the fathers, and the brothers, who are all eager to end his gallant career. The marquis is always in some difficulty because he is either constantly in love or loved by someone. The hilarious account of his slavery, entitled "The too accomplished slave," enables us to easily understand this statement: "Never has anyone been so happy as I in my servitude" (IV, 165). After being bought in the market place by his first master, he is taken home and immediately begins to court all of the women. The unhappy master then takes his charming slave and sells him on the spot. As a result of his charm, his abilities, and his intelligence he is passed from master to master, always happy and never kept. He finally arrives in Constantinople, from where he eventually leaves with Isabelle and Justinian.

Another of his stories concerns the time he poses as an astrologer, and this tale has served as the inspiration for a play by Thomas Corneille.[10] Here, too, he utilizes his imagination and his great sense of humor with quite entertaining results. He willingly explains the reasons for his attitude, and portrays himself in these

terms: "It is certain that I am inconstant, but at the same time I am
not troublesome. I never contradict anyone's opinions or stand in
the way of his pleasures. I give to others the freedom that I would
have them accord me. I do not find fault with constancy, although I
myself am happier with change, and my soul is so passionate that I
could never condemn anything connected with love" (II, 48).

He is interested in psychology and explains, in accordance with
the theory of the four humors, that one's temperament is dominated
by one of them: "It causes us to behave as it wishes; we are serious
or joyful, angry or patient, insensitive or impassionate, and it is not
so much because a melancholiac's mistress has been insensitive that
he spends his time in weeping, in constantly sighing, and in being
unable to sleep. . . . It goes without saying that if this same insen-
sitivity were directed at a man of my humor it would be received in
a different manner. The cheerfulness and the joy that come from
one's own nature are not easily affected by external matters" (II, 51).

The marquis is the life of the party, and knows an endless number
of ways to amuse a group of people. He is a master of conversation,
of description, and of psychology. Psychology, as a matter of fact,
plays an important role in the novel, and problems of a psychological
order provide the central theme for two other subplots.

Horace and Hyppolite are in love. Hyppolite (both a female and a
male name in the seventeenth century) is jealous of all other
women, except those old enough to have white hair (II, 246).
Horace, on the contrary, is not jealous of anyone. Even though
Hyppolite has many suitors, Horace remains serene, and this
arouses the young woman's anger. The following dialogue results, in
which Horace explains why he is not jealous:

HORACE: I know how to love properly and I respect you.
HYPPOLITE: Respect can be considered a sign of admiration and not necessarily a mark of love.
HORACE: If I no longer respected you, I would stop trusting you. Then I
would be worried and jealous.
HYPPOLITE: If you stopped being so indifferent, you would learn how to
really love. (IV, 45)

Their friends, however, are able to convince Hyppolite that she is
truly loved, and she finally marries Horace.

In the *Histoire de Léonide* it is the man, Alphonse, who is the
jealous one. Although he is sincerely loved, he is jealous of a dead

man. Alphonse is in love with Léonide, a widow who never loved the old husband her parents imposed upon her. She loved Octave, a friend from childhood, and when she marries someone else he is inconsolable and leaves to seek his death. Léonide regrets "having obeyed her father rather than having been faithful to the one she loved" (IV, 128).

The passing of time, however, heals her wounds and she meets Alphonse, whom she finds attractive, and even reminiscent of Octave. Léonide wants to forget her former love for Octave and does not mention it to Alphonse. Unfortunately, he learns of the story from someone else and is convinced that what Léonide loves in him is nothing more than the reflection of her former lover, Octave. Alphonse is then overcome by a frightful and annoying melancholy. When he complains of this to Léonide she answers him without pity: "He who imposes unnecessary problems upon himself cannot complain because he is the sole cause of whatever ills befall him" (IV, 146). Léonide, however, is a very determined woman and she declares her love for him in such a passionate manner that Alphonse is convinced of the error of his ways. At the end of the novel they, too, are married.

The story concerning the Comte de Lavagne is, in part, a free adaptation of an Italian work by Mascardi. It deals with both politics and ambition. The comte has been raised by an ambitious mother who wants to develop his political talents, but this is done to the detriment of ethical values. He is taught that if one has the ability to govern, nothing should stand in his way. One of his tutors explains that "among private citizens it is prudent not to rise above the average" (III, 423). This, however, does not apply to men of state. He also explains that "nature has endowed certain men with the qualities that are needed to enable them to obtain the glory to reign over all the others" (III, 421). Convinced that he possesses these attributes, the comte plots to assassinate all those who could prevent him from taking power. Just when he has succeeded in his plan, he falls from a boat and disappears below the water, carried down by the heavy weight of his armor. The lesson learned here is clear. The king is above his subjects, but he has been placed there by God, and it is evil to try to attain this position by one's own means. Mlle de Scudéry never wavered from this opinion, not during the reign of Louis XIII nor that of Louis XIV. She was as loyal to her king during the difficulties of the *Fronde* as during the splendor of his reign at Versailles.

There are three stories that concern Persians and Turks, and they contain more adventures and less psychology. The story about Roxelane, the sultan's wife, is closely tied to the main plot. Mlle de Scudéry first tells us the story of her parents. Her father, Bajazet, is a favorite of the sultan until he is given the task of going to Persia to fetch a beautiful slave who has been given as a present to Suleiman. When he sees her he immediately falls in love and decides to keep her for himself. Since she is Persian and speaks no Turkish, she does not understand what is happening. Bajazet then brings Alicola, one of his own wives, to the sultan to take the place of the beautiful slave. Alicola is quite beautiful, but she is also ambitious and quite proud. Her beauty pleases the sultan, but he finds her too haughty, and gives her as a gift to none other than Bajazet. Alicola, however, reveals the truth to Suleiman, and Bajazet is sent into exile along with the beautiful slave.

They have a daughter, Roxelane, who Bajazet hopes one day will be accepted into the sultan's harem so that he can regain his former position. As she is growing up, ambition is the only passion that is allowed to develop in her soul. Her father gives her advice of this type: "Any road that can take us where we want to go is the right one. Don't trouble yourself in asking if what you do is just, but only if it is advantageous" (II, 363). Educated in this fashion, Roxelane manages to become the sultan's favorite, avoids the intrigues of the harem, where everyone is jealous of her, and finally succeeds in marrying Suleiman. Since it is contrary to Turkish custom for a slave to marry the sultan it is clear that it has been brought about by a clever ruse.

Roxelane knows that the sultan loves her very much, and that because of this she has a great deal of power over him. She pretends to be going through a religious crisis and wishes to build a mosque. She consults a mufti and says that she is concerned about her chances for a second life. If she builds a mosque would it better her chances? She receives the answer that she had been expecting. No, because a slave cannot have a second life. She then feigns a profound sadness, and when Suleiman learns the cause he grants Roxelane her freedom. Now, of course, the trap has been well set because another consultation with the mufti reveals that the sultan "cannot possess" a free woman without marrying her (II, 381). Incapable of giving her up, Suleiman goes through with a marriage that is contrary to custom.

Once married, and a sultana, Roxelane becomes quite arrogant. She banishes those who displease her and poisons those who seem dangerous to her. She is able to maintain the sultan's love, and even though there are some passing infidelities, he always returns to her. The only jealousy she feels is toward Ibrahim's political influence, and she wants him dead. When, at the end of the novel, she learns that he has departed free and happy and that Rustan has been lynched, she "dies in a frenzied rage" (IV, 393).

The story of Osman and Alibech is told in two episodes and is concerned with pirates and love. Alibech's father, Arsalon, is a former Persian official at the court who fell into disgrace and then became a pirate. After having spent her youth in a school in Cyprus, Alibech has joined her father on the pirate ship. When Arsalon takes Osman prisoner, Alibech falls in love with the young man. Arsalon does not want to give him his freedom and so the young girl frees him herself. They escape together and make their way back to Constantinople, where Osman's father is a person of importance. He refuses to allow his son to marry Alibech because she has nothing to bring to the marriage. The sultan, who takes pity on the young girl, solves the problem by "adopting" her and by providing the dowry that makes her acceptable to the young man's father. The second part of the story takes place later. Arsalon, who was enraged by his daughter's elopement, has captured Osman's father and will not set him free unless his daughter returns to him. Alibech is ready to sacrifice herself, but Osman cannot bear to lose her, and they arrive at the pirate ship together. Arsalon is deeply moved by this sight and he frees everyone. Suleiman obtains a pardon for him and he gives up his career as a pirate.

The third story is about Axiamire, a young princess from Persia. Because of its complexity, with its mistaken identities, murders, and abductions, this tale would be impossible to describe in detail. Two of the characters, however, are especially worth mentioning: Axiamire herself, and the woman who gives us the only example of maternal love in all Mlle de Scudéry's works.

Axiamire is a well-depicted example of an independent woman who is impervious to love. Giangir, one of the sultan's sons, loves her, and though she has some affection for him, she confesses: "I am not capable of feeling this passion that unsettles the mind, destroys all reason and which robs the soul of its peace. I would prefer that Giangir had less passionate feelings for me" (III, 174). At the end of

the novel Giangir commits suicide because he unintentionally pro-
vokes his brother's execution, and Axiamire returns to Persia where
she helps her blind brother to reign. She promises to be "his guide"
and never to marry or to abandon him (IV, 308).

In the same story there is the example of the forementioned
maternal love. Roxelane has succeeded in having Suleiman order the
execution of his son Mustapha. This leads to the death of Mustapha's
brother Giangir, and paves the way for her son Mahomet's succes-
sion to the throne. Mustapha, however, has a son of his own, and
the mother, realizing the danger that her young son is in, tries to
flee with him to a safer place. Roxelane sends some men to overtake
them, and they succeed in abducting the child. The mother's chariot
has been sabotaged and she is forced to follow the abductors on foot.
She finally arrives to find her child murdered, and unable to bear
her intolerable sorrow, she slumps to her death on his body. This is
the most touching moment in the novel, and is especially memora-
ble because it is not in Mlle de Scudéry's customary style.

This first novel does foretell, however, the general style that will
dominate *Cyrus* and *Clélie*. They, too, will contain many adventures, psychological analyses, discussions about love, and character
portraits. It is also interesting to note the importance of feminism in
this novel. Although Ibrahim has a certain grandeur of his own,
Suleiman is little more than a puppet in the hands of the other
personages. The women, such as Isabelle, Roxelane, and Alibech,
among others, are given an importance that represents the role that
women played in French society at the time.

## II    Artamène ou Le Grand Cyrus

### A. *Structure*

This extremely successful novel in ten volumes was published by
Courbé between 1649 and 1653. In his *Bibliothèque françoise*, Sorel
summed up the reasons for its extraordinary popularity with the
reading public: "It is a book filled with heroic adventures in which
actions of love are pleasantly mixed with deeds of valor. With the
many examples of the gallantry of our century, and the exceedingly
charming conversations, there are hardly any readers who are not
moved by this work."[11] The book is attractive in a variety of ways,
mixing the charm of conversations on subjects that greatly interested the *précieux* with portraits of contemporary celebrities. All

of this is placed in an historical setting with heroes whose names are known to all.

The action, as in the case of *Ibrahim*, takes place in the Orient, but the historical period is a much earlier one. The story deals with the legendary Cyrus, who in the sixth century B.C., had conquered nearly all of Asia. Because of the remoteness of historical facts, the data concerning the period are confusing and sometimes contradictory. Historians such as Herodotus, Diodorus Siculus, or Justin have all written of Cyrus in conflicting terms. Mlle de Scudéry explains in the preface that this allowed her to choose what was most convenient for the composition of the novel. Furthermore, she jokingly points out at the end of the preface that the readers "can put their minds at rest by imagining that the sources for the work have been taken from an old Greek manuscript by Hegesippus which is in the Vatican library, and which is so precious and rare that it has never been printed, nor will it ever be" (I, 40).

One of the traditions has Cyrus dying as a result of a conflict with Thomiris, queen of the Massagetae. She was so furious over the death of her son that she had Cyrus beheaded and then dunked his head in a goatskin filled with blood. Mlle de Scudéry did not want to eliminate such a grandiose episode from her novel, but on the other hand she also could not have her hero killed. She then created Spitridate, an exact double of Cyrus. There are numerous scenes of mistaken identity, one of which has Spitridate's mother taking Cyrus for her own son, thus establishing the remarkable resemblance between the two. This explains how, at the end, Thomiris is able to make the same mistake.

Besides Cyrus' heroism and the magnitude of his victories, Mlle de Scudéry has also included other known facets of his character, such as his religious tolerance. For the rest of his personality she has borrowed greatly from Xenophon, whose *Cyropaedia* already had depicted Cyrus as the infallible hero.

The historical framework is rather loosely established by allusions to famous personages of the epoch such as Croesus, Sappho, Pisistratus or Solon, who are sometimes mixed in with the various adventures. Certain celebrated monuments are also mentioned, including the Hanging Gardens of Babylon, the Temple of Artemis at Ephesus, or the Temple of Apollo at Delphi, where one went to consult the Pythia. A reference to Gyges' ring, which was supposed to have properties that could render its wearer invisible, was actually utilized in the plot. Mlle de Scudéry has Mandane pass through the midst of an army thanks to the power of the fabled heliotrope stone that had been given to her just for the occasion.

The use of incredible events, which Mlle de Scudéry criticized in the preface of *Ibrahim*, is evident in *Cyrus*, although she has exercised some moderation. Since the action takes place either near a sea or a river, there are storms, shipwrecks, and pirates. However, the artifice that has been the most criticized, and not without reason, is the excessive use of abductions in this work. In fact, Princess Mandane is successively abducted by four of her suitors. For example, on one occasion Cyrus goes off to fight a duel, leaving the princess in the hands of a trustworthy soldier who turns out to be none other than a disguised prince who is in love with Mandane and who loses no time in abducting her.

It is to be noted, however, that in accordance with novelistic conventions of the time, his audacity goes no further. He will carry her off violently in his chariot or to a ship especially prepared for the daring event, but he will die of love and desperation because of the severity of the young girl who, despite everything, remains true to Cyrus.

It is not difficult to laugh, as Boileau did, at the warrior-hero, who does not hesitate to put his country to the torch, to cause bloodshed, and sometimes even to lose his crown for the love of a woman, only to behave in her presence afterwards like a lovesick adolescent. Even though this is difficult to believe, it is, nevertheless, part of the rules of the game, and this includes, of course, the hero's invincibility. Cyrus, however, does make some mistakes, and he does experience some minor defeats. At the beginning of the novel, for example, his generosity results in the escape of his prisoner. He is, at the time, serving under an assumed name in the army of King Ciaxare, Mandane's father. The king, believing him to be the escaped prisoner's accomplice, places Cyrus in prison.

On another occasion Cyrus is returning from a diplomatic mission and is unaware that Mandane has been abducted. He finds a man being attacked by several others and defends him valiantly. He does not know that he is unwittingly aiding the escape of the very one who has abducted Mandane (II, 290). These mistakes are evidently due to his generosity and his grandeur. He is even defeated in his first battle, albeit honorably. He and his friends are aboard a boat that attacks the fleet of the noble pirate Thrasibule. Despite an heroic battle that ends in the water with the wounded Cyrus still fighting against a man stronger than he, the inevitable takes place and he is taken prisoner. The pirate is so impressed with his grandeur that he pays him homage (I, 179) and, after caring for his wounds, sets him free.

During the wars Cyrus is taken prisoner twice, but both times he succeeds in hiding his identity. He is able, therefore, to extricate himself from rather difficult situations, all of which causes him to appear more human. Despite his heroism he still is susceptible of being defeated or of being imprisoned.

The novel, with its abductions, mishaps, and extraordinarily sudden changes, sometimes takes on the aspect of a serial. At the end of most volumes the hero finds himself in a seemingly insoluble situation, and the reader is left in utter suspense. The end of Volume VIII is characteristic of this. Mandane has been abducted by a man everyone believes to be Anaxaris, a simple officer. Indathirse knows the true identity of the abductor and reveals the name to Cyrus. "Cyrus separated himself from the rest of his troops, and marching quickly so as not to lose any time, listened to what Indathirse had to say to him. The look of astonishment on his face made it easy to realize that he had been greatly surprised and greatly distressed" (VIII, 778). The reader, therefore, curious to know who has abducted Mandane, must wait for the appearance of the ninth volume to learn that Anaxaris was really Aryante, Queen Thomiris' brother.

## B. *Main Plot*

The story begins with the capture of Sinope. The city is in flames and the assailants help the besieged to put out the rampaging fire. Cyrus, who has assumed the name of Artamène, has taken the city in order to free his beloved Mandane, who has been abducted and made prisoner by the king of Assyria. Upon entering the city, however, Cyrus learns that the unfortunate girl has been abducted again, this time by Prince Mazare, who she thought was merely trying to free her. The prince, however, is in love with Mandane and takes her to his ship. While at sea a terrible storm destroys the vessel and Mandane is lost.

Upon hearing this terrible news the grief-stricken Artamène goes to the seashore to search for Mandane's body. "After having looked in vain, he sat himself upon a rock jutting out into the water as if to wait for the waves to return to him what they had stolen" (I, 51).

When King Ciaxare, Mandane's father, learns of what has happened, and that his daughter's first abductor has been able to escape because Artamène, being too trustworthy, had not guarded him closely enough, he places the unhappy warrior in prison. Artamène refuses to answer the king's questions because in order to respond to them he would be obliged to reveal that he was really Cyrus, that Mandane had known his real identity, and that they had loved each other.

While not divulging this information, which certainly would have been painful for Ciaxare, Cyrus somewhat arrogantly maintains his innocence: "It is not easy to think of what could corrupt the fidelity of one who can dispose of crowns at his own will" (I, 74). This is in reference to the fact that by his services to Ciaxare he has been able to save him his throne.

Cyrus-Artamène is not concerned over appearing to be guilty because he knows well that he is not: "Ciaxare can think me to be cowardly and perfidious as much as he wants. It is not important to me as long as I, myself, know that I am not. . . . When we know the truth in our own consciences it is unnecessary to be troubled about anything else" (I, 80–81).

His friends are disturbed by the situation and by his silence, but they are also convinced that there is a good reason that justifies it. Féraulas and Chrysante, who have been Cyrus' companions since childhood, decide to disclose his disguise and the events that have led to the present predicament. He who is known by the name of Artamène is really Cyrus, the son of the king and queen of Persia. His mother is the sister of King Ciaxare, thus making him the king's nephew and the cousin of Mandane, whom he loves.

Since the oracles had announced that Cyrus, who was born at the court of his grandfather Astyage, would one day conquer all of Asia, the king, worried about the future of his reign, wants to have the infant killed. He is saved, however, and is raised by shepherds. He eventually is recognized by his grandfather, who succumbs to the young boy's charm and abandons his plan to have him killed. Cyrus is sent to his parents' court in Persia, where he receives the type of education that permits him to develop into an accomplished young man.

As the grandfather grows older he becomes very jealous and has Cyrus closely watched. On the other hand, the young man is impatient to leave the court in order that he may set out on his own: "I want to learn from traveling. I want the opportunity to prove myself. I want to learn about myself, and, if possible, I want the whole world to know my name" (I, 152). He then secretly leaves his father's court in the company of Chrysante and Féraulas. In order to appease his grandfather's jealousy, he lets it be known that he has been killed in a shipwreck, and begins to travel under the assumed name of Artamène.

During one of his voyages, a storm at sea causes him to be thrown ashore in Cappadocia, a territory belonging to Ciaxare, the son of Astyage. Even though he, too, is an enemy, Cyrus travels to his uncle's court at Pteria, where it is highly improbable that anyone can recognize him. It is there that he sees Mandane for the first time. Ironically, she is attending a sacrificial ceremony offered each year to the gods thanking them for Cyrus' death. The young man changes color at the sight of the beautiful Mandane, and falls passionately in love with her. He decides to stay at court, incognito, safely hidden under the name of Artamène. On several occasions he covers himself with glory and even saves Ciaxare's life, thus winning the esteem of both father and daughter.

Before leaving for still another battle, Cyrus entrusts Féraulas with a letter in which he respectfully declares his love for the princess, and although he does not reveal his true identity, he does admit that he is not unworthy of her. He asks Féraulas to deliver the letter in the event that he should die, so that Mandane would be aware of the noble feelings she had aroused in him.

Cyrus is wounded in the battle and when he takes refuge in a certain castle, he is believed to be dead. This episode is doubly important because he is in the castle of a princess who is his double's mother. When she immediately believes that the wounded man is her son Spitridate, we learn for the first time of the existence of someone who resembles Cyrus in every way. In the meantime, Féraulas has delivered Cyrus' letter of farewell to Mandane. Believing him to be dead, she allows herself to speak of her feelings, and confesses: "I now realize that Artamène had a larger place in my heart than I thought. . . . My soul is troubled, and I feel a pain beginning to possess me. I know that despite what I felt before, the certainty of his love does not offend me" (II, 72).

The unusual circumstances surrounding the revelation of Cyrus' love prevented Mandane from having the normal reaction to such a declaration. In Mlle de Scudéry's novels a woman was obliged to be quite severe when confronted with the audacity of a man who dared to aspire to her love. When Cyrus recovers from his wounds and returns to court, Mandane is happy to see him again, but she finds herself in a difficult situation because her love for the hero is known to Féraulas, who reports it, of course, to Cyrus. Propriety demands that she hide her feelings until he has proven himself to be a faithful suitor and worthy of her love. Mandane explains her problem to her confidante Martésie: "If I had to banish Artamène it would not be without a certain repugnance, and it would cause me a great amount of pain. However, in consideration of my self-esteem it is important that Artamène not have suspicion of my weakness. I have told him many kind things and I fear that he will have thoughts I do not wish him to have. I would prefer that both of us suffer rather than risk losing his respect" (II, 156).

Cyrus is able, however, to convince her of his respect and of the profound love he feels for her. When he reveals his identity she is happy because he is actually a great prince for whom the oracles have promised an extremely glorious future. Mandane is also afraid of what steps her father and her still jealous grandfather, Astyage, might take if they knew that Cyrus was alive. She then imposes these conditions on Cyrus: "I find your conversation quite pleasing and the manner in which you express your love completely satisfies my virtue, but, nevertheless, I am obliged to tell you that if you are unable in three months (and I fear that even this period of time is unseemly) to find a way to bring Cyrus back to life without risk of danger, I will have you return to Persia and live happily if you can, no longer thinking about the unhappy Mandane if this should disturb your peace" (II, 168).

Cyrus is delighted with the reprieve that he has been granted, and he thinks to avail himself of Mandane's presence during this time. However, King Astyage has convinced his son, who is a widower, to remarry, and he suggests that the beautiful Thomiris, the queen of the Massagetae and a widow, would make a fine match. Ciaxare then decides to send the one whom he believes to be Artamène as ambassador to ask for the queen's hand. Despite the separation that this voyage imposes on him and his beloved Mandane, Cyrus is happy to have been chosen for the task because he thinks that if he is successful it might help him to win Ciaxare's acceptance of his true identity.

His hopes, however, are shattered because Queen Thomiris falls hopelessly in love with him at first sight. Cyrus is greatly troubled because he does not want to be disrespectful of the queen, but on the other hand he absolutely cannot be unfaithful to Mandane: "I swear that this bizarre adventure displeases me, and if I had my choice I would rather fight two battles than find myself with the insupportable necessity of shaming such a glorious and proud queen" (II, 242). Thomiris finally offers him the crown, placing herself in a situation not unlike the scene between Phèdre and Hippolyte, where in both cases the young man pretends to have not understood. Cyrus answers the queen in this manner: "O Madam! I have doubtlessly misunderstood, and I feel that because of the great respect that is your due I dare not answer" (II, 251).

Thomiris refuses, however, to accept Cyrus' indifference and will not allow him to depart. He must then escape from the amorous queen's court and return to report his failure to King Ciaxare. His concern over what the king will say turns into despair when he learns that in his absence Mandane has been abducted by the king of Assyria. Cyrus leads an army in the pursuit of the abductor, who has taken refuge in Babylon.

When the city is taken Cyrus is unable to rejoin Mandane because she and the king had escaped before the siege began. He now follows their trail to Sinope, where he finds the city in flames, and it is at this point that the novel begins. As has already been mentioned, Mazare abducts Mandane from the king of Assyria and takes her to his boat that eventually sinks at sea, thus causing Cyrus to believe that she is dead.

It is learned later that Mandane had been saved by the king of Pontus, who took her aboard his ship in the hope of winning her love. Ciaxare, who had imprisoned Artamène-Cyrus, now needs him to fight against the king of Pontus, and lets himself be persuaded to free him even though he learns from Féraulas that Artamène is really Cyrus.

After many perilous adventures, during which Mandane is convinced at one point that Cyrus has been untrue to her and loves Princess Araminte, the lovers are finally reunited at Cumae. The novel could easily end here. Mandane is rescued, Cyrus' identity is known, and his valor is such that Ciaxare cannot possibly oppose a marriage between the two young people. However, the novel takes off again, and Mlle de Scudéry manages to write two more volumes.

Cyrus had made a vow earlier to the king of Assyria that he would not marry Mandane without first fighting a duel with him. Now that nothing prevents him from marrying Mandane, he feels that he must keep his word and go through with the duel. This is quite chivalrous on his part because the king of Assyria had often broken his promises, but Cyrus, being the hero he is, cannot do likewise. Before leaving he entrusts Mandane to Anaxaris, who turns out to be Aryante, Queen Thomiris' brother and secretly in love with Mandane. He loses no time in carrying off the oft-abducted young woman, and takes her to Thomiris. She assures him of her protection if he renounces his claim to the throne, which he does.

Cyrus then pursues Aryante and Mandane and finally arrives at the camp of Queen Thomiris. There he is taken prisoner by one of her occasional allies, but is not delivered to the queen. When Spitridate, whom everyone takes for Cyrus, dies, Mandane is stricken with grief, but it is short-lived because she soon learns that it was not Cyrus who had been killed. Thomiris also discovers the truth and searches the camp until she finds Cyrus. Since he still refuses to marry her, she threatens to kill Mandane. At this point Cyrus' army arrives and he is once again reunited with his Mandane.

This time the novel really comes to an end, with the hero and heroine marrying at last. Just as the oracles had predicted, Cyrus reigns over all of Asia, and Mlle de Scudéry comments that he was a model sovereign who left behind many remarkable laws. He also mastered the art of innocent pleasures so well "that by staying in Babylon during the autumn and winter, in Susa during the spring, and in Ecbatana during the summer, he was able to live in an eternal springtime, feeling neither the great discomfort of the cold nor that of the heat" (X, 850). It can be noted that Cyrus had accomplished what seems to have been one of Mlle de Scudéry's dreams.

## C. *Subplots*

Each of the ten volumes is divided into three books, and each book, in turn, contains a minimum of one story or a maximum of four. These stories are either tied to the main plot, such as the story of Mazare (V, 370), and continue in the form of episodes until the end of the novel, or they can have little or no connection.

Love is always the principal theme of the secondary stories, and they vary mainly in their degree of complication. Some of them are extremely complex, others easily told in a few sentences. There are twenty-seven of them, and this large number precludes a complete résumé. Some, however, are so attractive that they are worth mentioning.

One of these is the story of Parthénie, the beginning of which relates the difficulties encountered by Mme de Sablé in her marriage. At first she is passionately loved by her husband, but he gradually estranges himself from her. Mlle de Scudéry is careful to explain why: "He loved Parthénie for her beauty alone, and when his eyes became accustomed to the sight of her, his passion diminished. His feelings slowly went from mild affection to indifference and from indifference to contempt. Since his manner was rather bizarre, their temperaments were not at all compatible" (VI, 103). The husband, however, defends his attitude in saying: "I find nothing more extravagant than to see a husband who is still in love with his wife. I don't know exactly what it is, but there is something in marriage that makes it incompatible with love, and I cannot tolerate that I am blamed if I no longer feel anything for Parthénie" (VI, 104).

Parthénie is so unhappy over the situation that she falls ill and loses her stunning beauty. She leaves for a refuge in the country and dedicates herself to study. Living alone, and in peace, she is gradually able to recover her past brilliance, and even after her husband's death she continues to live in solitude. An oracle predicts that she will find happiness again only if she is able to seduce a man without the help of her beauty. She thinks that this means the end of her romantic life, but she is mistaken.

One day she is singing in the midst of a labyrinthian garden, and Timante, who cannot find his way out, overhears her and is enchanted with the sound of her voice. Parthénie finds this amusing and wishes to prolong the game. She grants Timante a rendezvous in which she is completely veiled. This only adds to the young man's fascination and curiosity. In an effort to make him believe that she is terribly ugly, Parthénie tells Timante that if he promises not to speak to her he can see her at church the following day. She then sends in her place a servant of the same height but with an absolutely monstrous face. The lovesick Timante is horrified at first, but he soon realizes that the monster does not have his beloved's hands and he is reassured.

Parthénie has little confidence in her possibilities for happiness and would like nothing better than to break off relations with Timante without revealing either her name or her face. Fortunately, her family intervenes, and the story ends happily when Timante is invited to visit Princess Parthénie whose beauty he had admired from afar. This wonderful scene comes to a close when the ecstatic

Timante hears her voice and realizes that Princess Parthénie and his beloved *inconnue* are one and the same.

The story of Sésostris and Timarète, which takes place in Egypt, is also found in the sixth volume. As in the case of *Paul et Virginie*, Sésostris and Timarète learn to love each other at an early age. They grow up on a small island in the Nile where they are able, nevertheless, to receive a fine education that will later permit them, after they are elevated to their proper rank, to marry and rule Egypt. Mlle de Scudéry has painted a charming picture of their young love:

Sésostris could not bear to be away from Timarète for very long, and he never indulged in disputes with her, giving in on all matters, despite being at an age when compliance is rare. If she remarked that she needed some rattan stems for the baskets in which she placed fruit, he went diligently to gather them for her. If she expressed a desire for flowers he could not rest until he had brought her some bouquets, and he dreamt so much of pleasing her that he thought of little else. For her part, Timarète was kind to everyone who saw her, but her way with Sésostris was so notably different that it was difficult not to be aware of it. (VI, 365–66)

Sésostris has the opportunity to demonstrate his courage when he saves Timarète from the claws of an enormous crocodile. Armed only with a shepherd's staff, the young boy struggles with the monster, which almost takes on the proportions of a dragon. When the crocodile stands on its hind legs, Sésostris stabs it in a place where there are no scales, and pierces the heart. This battle, which is obviously not accurately described from a scientific point of view, gives a great deal of pleasure to Sésostris, who feels "glorified from his victory" and even has the elegance to ask Timarète's pardon for having taken so long to kill the beast.

After many adventures Sésostris is recognized as the legitimate king of Egypt and marries Timarète. Her father had usurped the throne and, now growing old, he gives up the crown in order to ease his guilty conscience.

Some of the subplots are meant to illustrate a theory. In the third volume unhappiness is discussed, and Mandane's confidante, Martésie, listens to a story about some *"amants infortunés"* and then must decide who suffers the most: the absent lover, the lover not loved, the lover in mourning, or the jealous lover. Martésie gives an opinion that recognizes the pain of each, but awards the prize to the lover in mourning, whose story is truly pitiful (III, 328).

D. *The Portraits*

Cyrus generated so much interest and curiosity that a key to its characters was published in 1657, four years after the publication of the final volumes. Since that time it has been common knowledge that Cyrus was a portrayal of the Prince de Condé, and that his sister, Mme de Longueville, to whom the novel is dedicated, was depicted as Mandane. Mlle de Scudéry used the *Cyropaedia* as a general framework for Cyrus's portrayal as a king, but many other facets of his character were representative of Condé as a young man. Michelet's epithet in regard to Condé, *"Ce héros à la Corneille,"* has often been repeated, and Cyrus does in fact greatly resemble Rodrigue in his courage and enthusiasm. Mandane herself makes an allusion to one of the most quoted lines from *Le Cid* (II, 2), when she says to the young prince: "I do not know if you have won without peril, but I know well that you have not triumphed without glory" (I, 302).

Cyrus' noble bearing shows that he is a man meant for victory: "The prince was quite tall and well-proportioned. His face was very handsome, and all of the artifices used by the Medes to beautify their hair could not approach what nature alone had done for his. Its color was of the most beautiful brown in the world, and it fell charmingly in natural curls to his shoulders. His coloring was vivid, and his dark eyes were filled with vivacity, sweetness, and majesty" (III, 343). When he approached battle "it was said that a new spirit overcame him and that he himself became the god of war" (V, 290).

His treatment of Mandane is always gallant and respectful, and from the moment they meet, it is for her that he seeks glory as a warrior. At one time Mandane judges him unjustly, but Cyrus never once departs from his perfect attitude toward her. His behavior toward Thomiris is perhaps even more remarkable. Even though she has acted in an undignified way, Cyrus continues to treat her with the respect due a woman and a queen. The question of whether or not a woman should, as Thomiris does, be the first to declare her love is discussed. It is decided that the problem is ambiguous because even if propriety does not allow a woman to act in this manner, nature has created men and women equal in matters of the heart and, therefore, it should make no difference who makes the first declaration of love.

As for Cyrus, the problem never arises. He loves Mandane at first sight and will never be interested in other women, although he treats them in a perfectly courteous manner. This extraordinary love that Cyrus has for Mandane, and the perfection of his behavior, is certainly not applicable to the rebel of the *Fronde* or the man who helped Bussy-Rabutin to abduct a woman. This incident has often been cited, but, even so, the portrait of Cyrus does undoubtedly retrace certain aspects of Condé's personality such as his heroism, pride, and tenderness. The latter was demonstrated in his feelings for Marthe du Vigean, whom he loved as a young man. Once as he was about to leave her to go to war, he fainted from the pain it caused him.[12] Mlle de Scudéry has assuredly chosen facets of his personality and events from his life that were compatible with the personage of the novel, and she conveniently eliminated the rest.

The same can be said of the treatment given Mandane. Mme de Longueville's blonde beauty and her extraordinary charm are well depicted, but there is no mention of her haughtiness, her romantic adventures, or her political errors during the *Fronde*. She seems to have been much admired by Mlle de Scudéry, who chose to overlook her faults, and she could be every bit as charming as Mandane when it was her wish. There is an interesting contrast between the ethereal image Mlle de Scudéry has drawn of Mme de Longueville and the pungent description of her that Bussy-Rabutin included in his *Histoire amoureuse des Gaules:* "The princess, who was dirty and who had an unpleasant odor, was also unable to hide other bad qualities. . . ."[13]

In the novel Mandane is physically, morally, and intellectually perfect. She has received an excellent education because it is she who will reign after Ciaxare's death. Since the laws of the kingdom forbid her to marry a foreign prince, and since there is no one in the realm of a birth high enough to aspire to her hand, it seems that she must remain celibate. Mandane's subjects, however, are so filled with admiration for her that they do not regret that the throne will one day be hers.

Mandane displays only one moment of imperfection, and this is when she believes Cyrus to have been unfaithful to her. He is laying siege to Sardis in an effort to free her, and instead of waiting for him she uses the magic ring of Gyges to pass, invisible, through his army, thus necessitating several other heroic exploits that are described in an additional volume. At long last Cyrus is able to convince Mandane of his fidelity, and despite the fact that he is a Persian, they are allowed to marry because "the conqueror of all Asia is a foreigner nowhere" (X, 840).

Condé and Mme de Longueville are the most vividly drawn

characters in *Cyrus,* but the novel does contain numerous other portraits. Christina of Sweden, is presented as Princess Cléobuline, and the Comte de Chabot, Condé's best friend, is seen as Féraulas. Among many others pictured in the novel are Mme de Maure, Mlle de Vandy, and Mme des Pennes. Volume seven contains the story of Elise, which is a portrayal of Mlle Paulet, *"La Lionne de l'Hôtel de Rambouillet."* This gives Mlle de Scudéry the opportunity to provide the reader with a veritable gallery of portraits depicting many of the celebrated guests of this renowned salon. Mme de Rambouillet is portrayed as Cléomire, and her two daughters Angélique and Julie are represented as Anacrise and Philonide. Julie's pleasant personality is well described, and her passion for enjoying herself is succinctly summed up in this comment: "I do not think that she has ever been indisposed on a day when there was a party to attend" (VII, 301). Portraits of Conrart, Chapelain, Mme Aragonnais, Mme Cornuel, Montausier, Isarn, and many others are found in various episodes throughout the novel.

The most famous portraits in the novel, however, are the ones that Mlle de Scudéry draws of herself and of Pellisson. They are represented as Sapho and Phaon, and their relationship gives Mlle de Scudéry an opportunity to express her feelings about platonic love. This notion, first suggested by the French marquis in *Ibrahim,* is much more clearly stated in *Cyrus,* and will culminate in *Clélie* with the *Carte de Tendre.* Although the marquis is quite fickle, in *Cyrus* the theory of a spiritual love that lasts an entire lifetime is clearly set forth. When they are apart Phaon is perfectly able to amuse himself, while Sapho can only suffer in his absence. This could lead to an irreparable disagreement between the two because of Sapho's jealousy and her belief that Phaon has been unfaithful to her. They then decide to leave Lesbos together and go to live in the land of the *Nouveaux Sauromates,* where the citizens are held together mainly by laws concerning love. Judging from a description, one could say that this is the land of *Préciosité.* This is what one of the Sauromates says about his country: "All of the customs concerning lovers are as old as the state itself and are as inviolable as those regarding religion. One cannot change mistresses without giving the reason why, and mistresses are bound to do the same if they wish to change. Our existence is made up mainly of peace, leisure time, and abundance, and we speak only of love in all of our conversations" (X, 574).

Mlle de Scudéry is summing up at this point the particular conditions that were prevalent in the *société précieuse*. Leisure time and wealth allowed the *précieuses* to live a life free from material exigencies, and, as a result, they could devote themselves entirely to *galanterie*.

Since all questions of a sentimental nature are decided by judges, Phaon asks for a ruling that will oblige Sapho, who does not wish to marry, at least to give him the hope that one day she will change her mind. "But Sapho adroitly argued that in order to love forever, and with an equal ardor, it was necessary not to marry. The judges were so impressed that they forbade Phaon to press the point, stating that it was a favor that Sapho alone could grant, and he should consider himself the happiest and most glorious suitor on earth to be loved by the most perfect person in the world" (X, 607).

Love and marriage and a woman's place in society are often the subjects of conversations found throughout Mlle de Scudéry's novels, and an entire chapter will be dedicated to their analysis. Besides conversations and character portrayals, which were of great interest to readers of the time, *Cyrus* also offers secondary stories that are actually novels in themselves. These stories are extremely varied, taking place in Asia, Greece, or in Gaul at the time of the Druids, and could be greatly enjoyed by the modern reader. Perhaps the most attractive element of this novel, however, is the personnage of Cyrus himself. With his youth, enthusiasm, and courage he represents the type of hero whose appeal is universal and timeless.

### III   Clélie

#### A. *Historical Setting*

This ten–volume novel was published by Augustin Courbé between the years 1654 and 1661. Mlle de Scudéry, as was the custom, and as was expected of her by her public, fashioned a mixture of historical events with imaginary ones. She recounts several stories of love and discusses gallant casuistry, all based on a foundation of historical truth. Clélie was one of the most renowned heroines of ancient Rome, and the names Horatius, Mutius, Brutus, and Lucrèce were all familiar to those who had studied Roman history. In order to be on firm ground Mlle de Scudéry uses several pages (II, 834–61) to retrace the history of Rome from its beginnings to the establishment of the Republic, the period during which the events narrated in the story took place.[14]

It is quite evident that before writing the novel she did extensive research because the indications of her knowledge of Roman history are abundant. She was not content with the brief mention of Clélie on Manlius' shield that appeared in the *Aeneid*, but read very closely the first two volumes of Livy's *History of Rome*, Plutarch's *The Parallel Lives* (in the celebrated translation by Amyot), and *Roman Antiquities* of Dionysius of Halicarnassus.

A novelist's objective was not to depict history as it actually happened, but to utilize a well-known period of history as a backdrop, and then, through one's inventive ability, stimulate the reader's imagination. Almost everyone knew of this particularly glorious period in Roman history, when in the sixth century B.C. the citizens, led by Brutus, heroically deposed the kings and established a republic. Starting with an astonishingly solid historical basis, despite what Boileau might have thought, Mlle de Scudéry eliminated "base and vulgar matters" (VIII, 1131), which she felt would have displeased her readers. For example, Horatius is historically known as *Cocles* or "one eye." Mlle de Scudéry delicately omits this unpleasant detail and transforms Horatius into a handsome lover impassioned of Clélie, conserving, nevertheless, all the legendary heroics that are attributed to him.

Mlle de Scudéry gives some extremely accurate and precise descriptions in the novel, such as the topographical picture she paints of Rome at the end of the monarchy. She also describes a method of divination called the Praenestine Lots, which is in agreement with Cicero's description from his *De Divinatione* (II, 41).[15] This practice, which originated in the city of Praeneste over a century before, involved the random selection of pieces of wood with letters carved on them. The use of these details effectively creates an authenticity of atmosphere. At the same time, she has Clélie attend a ceremony with an ingenious adornment in diamonds that includes a secret compartment for two portraits. This type of anachronism shocks our present-day taste for historical precision, but for Mlle de Scudéry it was merely part of the rules of the game that, moreover, represented an added charm for her readers.

## B. *Principal Plots*

The novel contains three principal plots. They are closely related and include the main characters that one encounters throughout the entire novel. The protagonists are Clélie and Aronce. The young girl is the daughter of Clélius, a Roman exiled because of his opposition

to Tarquin. He is a proud man, very patriotic, and will have only a
Roman as a son-in-law. Years before, during a terrible storm at sea,
he lost one of his children but found, at the same time, an infant in a
crib floating on the water. He names the child Aronce and raises
him as his own son. Having grown to adulthood, Aronce falls in love
with Clélie and is, in turn, loved by her. Clélius reluctantly con-
sents to their marriage because even though Aronce is not Roman
born, he has great prowess as a warrior and has saved Clélius' life on
several occasions. At this time it is conveniently learned that Aronce
is none other than the son of Princess Galérite and Porsenna, king of
Clusium. Porsenna is in prison, where he has been kept for twenty-
three years by his father-in-law, King Mézence. Aronce intends to
marry and then seek to free his father, but on the eve of the wedding
there is an earthquake that permits Horace, a Roman who is also in
love with Clélie, and who is preferred by Clélius as a prospective
son-in-law, to abduct the unhappy bride. In the pursuit that follows
Aronce has the opportunity to save the life of Mézence, his grandfather, and therefore gain his confidence. At precisely this time,
after twenty-three years of imprisonment, Porsenna is able to escape and regain his kingdom; and because of political reasons, he
forbids his son to marry Clélie, who is a Roman.

He allies himself with Tarquin, who is a haughty, cruel, and
authoritarian king and the husband of the proud Tullie. In order to
marry they had to eliminate, with the use of poison, their previous
spouses, who happened to be Tullie's sister and Tarquin's brother.
In doing so they were able, in one stroke, to satisfy their love and
their desire to rule together. Many Romans are sent into exile and
plot to overthrow Tarquin and Tullie. During this struggle Clélie,
who had been kidnapped by Horace, is now captured by Tarquin
and made prisoner. Unaware at first of her identity and that she is
the daughter of one of his worst enemies, he falls in love with her.
To make matters worse, Tarquin's son Sextus, as brutal as his father,
also falls in love with Clélie. When Tarquin finally learns the true
identity of his prisoner, despite his anger and desire to avenge
himself on Clélius by killing his daughter, he is unable to harm her
because of his great passion. She, in the meantime, continues to
pine for her beloved Aronce.

Tarquin's downfall is brought about by Brutus, who is related to
the regal family. After having been educated elsewhere, and realizing that his life might be in danger because any male of the royal

family is considered a threat by Tarquin, he feigns stupidity. Upon his return to court he is able to convince everyone that he is mentally retarded. This includes the wife that Tarquin chooses for him and the two sons that result from their union. They are unable to perceive the acute intelligence that Brutus is hiding and his great desire to free Rome from the yoke of tyranny that Tarquin has placed upon it.

Brutus' wife dies and he meets Lucrèce, a young girl who also believes him to be retarded. She learns through a poem that Brutus writes for her that he is only pretending to be backward in order to protect himself, and is secretly preparing for the liberation of Rome. Unfortunately, Lucrèce's father discovers a letter from Brutus that clearly establishes the true state of affairs, and in order to save her beloved she agrees to marry Collatin, chosen by her father. Once married she declares to Brutus that she no longer wishes to see him and that she will lead the life of a faithful wife, if not a loving one. She then moves to the country, apart from the world and in a solitude that befits her sadness.

Collatin invites some of his friends, among whom is Sextus, Tarquin's son, to visit his home in order to show off his lovely wife, of whom he is quite proud. Overcome by her beauty, Sextus returns to Lucrèce by himself and rapes her. She summons her husband and father, who are accompanied by Brutus, who suspects that something is terribly wrong. When they arrive she tells of Sextus' vile deed, proclaims her innocence, and, crying for vengeance, stabs herself to death. Brutus, choking with pain and rage, forgets his disguise, and cries out for all to avenge this outrage. The populace, convinced that Brutus has miraculously regained his senses, follows him and succeeds in overthrowing Tarquin. The Republic is established, but Tarquin, allied with Porsenna, tries to reconquer the city.

They lay siege to Rome, and when an armistice is arranged, Clélie is sent as a hostage to Porsenna's camp. The proud Tullie, anxious to help her husband, lies to Porsenna in the hope that he will continue the war against Rome. She even succeeds in convincing him that his son Aronce is a traitor, and so he is placed in prison.

Clélie has a dream in which Lucrèce appears to warn her about Sextus, who is planning to abduct her. She is advised to escape at once, and so she and her companions flee the camp and are able to reach Rome by swimming across the Tiber. Despite this heroic action, Clélie is forced to return to Porsenna's camp because of certain stipulations agreed upon in the armistice. Porsenna, however, is impressed with Rome's honesty and with Clélie's great charm. Since he has seen through Tullie's manipulations and has learned the proof of his son's innocence, he finally agrees to Aronce's marriage with Clélie and makes peace with Rome.

## C. Subplots

These subordinate stories, numbering twelve, are generally told to a group of the novel's principal characters. They are always different in length and style, and their subjects deal mainly with love, as can be seen in the following examples.

One of them concerns Herminius, a Roman opposed to Tarquin. He loves Valérie and is, in turn, loved by her. For political reasons he must go into exile, and at this time he encounters Clélie, for whom he has a *tendre amitié* (explained by the *Carte de Tendre*), but his feelings are mistaken for love. One of Herminius' friends, Emile, believing that Herminius is dead, returns to Rome, where he meets Valérie. Unaware of her relationship with Herminius, Emile tells her of his death and his supposed love for Clélie. Emile himself falls in love with Valérie and is able to persuade her to marry him because she now believes that Herminius is dead and has been unfaithful to her.

On the day of their marriage, however, Herminius returns and is able to prove that his relationship with Clélie has been nothing more than a "tender friendship." Valérie now finds herself in the position of being betrothed to two men. The political situation comes to their rescue and the two rivals for Valérie's hand are forced to flee Rome. At the end of the novel the Praenestine Lots affirm that Valérie should marry Herminius, whom she truly loves.

The story of Artaxandre is an *histoire à clé*. Artaxandre is actually the name that Amilcar, one of the secondary characters in the main plot, uses in relating two of his amorous adventures. He is an African traveling through Italy and becomes fond of Aronce. Artaxandre is gallant, charming, and is also a poet. Even if we do not have a precise key as to whom the characters in *Clélie* were fashioned after in real life, we do know from contemporary accounts that Artaxandre-Amilcar was supposed to be the poet Jean-François Sarasin, just as we know that Herminius was the namesake for Pellisson.

The first adventure concerns Pasithée, whom Artaxandre loves but abandons after having learned that she consoled herself much too soon after her previous lover's death. He then falls in love with the beautiful Cynésie, who returns his love, but he leaves her, too, because she allowed herself in the past to be courted by a man whom Artaxandre considers to be a fool. He would never tolerate courting a woman who could possibly be sensitive to the wooing of such a boor. Disappointed in these two unhappy attempts at love, he now dedicates himself to friendship and spreads joy wherever he goes. Amilcar is without a doubt the most beguiling personage in *Clélie*, and his name became synonymous with the type of man who was handsome, seductive, and gallant.

In the story of Artélise, the young girl has no fewer than four suitors. When she decides to marry the one who lets himself be accused of murder rather than reveal his nocturnal visits to his beloved's garden, the other three suitors are heartbroken and leave together to go to war. They call themselves the "lovers in mourning," and adopt the slogan, "we seek to die." Two of them find their desire realized in the sixth volume, and the third follows them in the eighth volume while defending his fallen comrades' tomb against a group of enemies.

In another story, Césonie feels that it is better to be loved than to love, and she marries Turnus whom she believes to be more passionately in love with her than Persandre, whom she prefers. She is mistaken in her choice, however, because once married, Turnus leaves her and departs on a long voyage. The faithful Persandre visits her often, and when she fears for her reputation, she insists that he marry. He obliges by taking the lovely Danaé as his wife. When Turnus returns he falls in love with Danaé, and the entire city becomes fascinated with this imbroglio, which is finally resolved when the two couples make an exchange. Since they are social equals, and have no children, a divorce is arranged, the women merely exchanging households. Césonie and Persandre are happy with the new arrangement, but Turnus, who married Danaé, falls in love once again with his ex-wife.

Plotine, a friend and confidante of Césonie, has suffered from jealousy because she believed the man she loved to have been untrue to her. Even when he is able to prove that her fears are unfounded, she declares herself unable to love him as before: "I could no longer summon up in my heart, even if I wanted to, this kind of love, filled as it is with an uneasy tenderness. The resentment I felt has chased it away and my good sense, having become stronger, will not allow it to return" (X, 1024).

Freed from her love, Plotine dedicates herself thereafter to her friends. However, when she meets Amilcar, whom she resembles in many ways, she forms a *tendre amitié* with him. Both of them are gallant, and both take great joy in giving zest to the conversations and games of their society. Amilcar's sudden death at the site of the Prenaestine Lots is reminiscent of the death of Jean-François Sarasin, and for Mlle de Scudéry it is also a way of conveniently ending this particular subplot. The once joyful Plotine, who previously took very little seriously, is so saddened by Amilcar's death that she falls ill and is unable to attend the marriage of Clélie and Aronce with which, in a burst of joy, the tenth and final volume of the novel concludes.

## D. *The Portraits*

Boileau was of the opinion that it was the presence of the portraits that assured the success of Mlle de Scudéry's novels. He felt that it was particularly true in the case of *Clélie*, which he considered to be a gallery of the *bourgeois* living in the Marais. According to him they read these books out of curiosity and were flattered to find themselves portrayed. Boileau admits that he, himself, had no definite knowledge of a key to the characters, and, in fact, there is no proof that any ever existed. One should surely not exaggerate the importance of these descriptions, interesting as they were to the reader. They were, for the most part, rather imprecise so as not to divulge the real identity of the person described. This was, of course, not the case with Mlle de Scudéry's immediate entourage who could, through subtle hints, readily guess who was being depicted.

For today's reader *Clélie*, as far as its characters are concerned, offers an insoluble puzzle. Except for the rare cases in which famous persons are described, such as Louis XIV, the future Mme de Maintenon, Scarron, Mme de Sévigné, the painter Nanteuil, Arnauld d'Andilly, and the *Solitaires de Port-Royal*, the reader of the twentieth century has little idea of the identity of the majority of the characters. As a matter of fact, the same could be said of Mlle de Scudéry's contemporaries.

In regard to the technique and the goal of character portrayals, Mlle de Scudéry gives a rather long explanation in Volume IX:

One should never reproach a person for a lack of beauty or for being unfortunate if one does not wish to seem cowardly or taunting. If unpleasant things are called for they must be said of those who are villains, scandal-mongers, slanderers, swindlers, and those envious of other persons' glory. In fashioning a good portrait of an evil man one can sometimes instill a loathing for vice. Above all, these portrayals must be general and not indicate anyone in particular unless it is necessary to expose those who are perfidious in order that they cannot deceive others. (IX, 294–95)

The goal of the portrait, then, is twofold: it describes, and it also offers a possible moral lesson. According to classical tradition, one should not describe a specific person and his defects but should rather describe specific defects and then apply them to a fictitious character. The reader might be somewhat disappointed in this technique because judging from some rare examples Mlle de Scudéry could be quite naughty when it struck her fancy.

An example of this can be seen when she plays at the game of the *portraits partagés*. First she gives us the customary portrait, which is rather vague and innocuous: "Amérinthe is tall, shapely, and has all the brilliance of great beauty. Her eyes sparkle and are alluring. They express love, fear, and hope at the same time" (IX, 288). The portrait continues in this tone, describing some physical attributes and mixing them with psychological commentaries. Nothing of a negative quality is ever mentioned.

In the second portrait, however, the positive aspects are repeated but are dealt with much more profoundly. The physical description starts pleasantly enough, but then it changes direction: "Her hair is blonde and her bearing is rather noble, but her hands will never win anyone's heart because they are so ugly. She is so afraid that they will be seen by her suitors that she hides them in a part of her veil. . . ." (IX, 290–91) Mlle de Scudéry then passes on to a psychological aspect of the character and concludes: "Finally, the truest thing that can be said of her is that no other person has inspired so much love and so much hate, and has attracted so much praise and so many insults. What is most annoying about this is that one always admires her at first but inevitably comes to the point of despising her" (IX, 292–93).

The *portraits partagés* are, unfortunately, only a game initiated at the court of Princess Lysimène, who is displeased with them and discourages the practice. Mlle de Scudéry approves of her attitude: "It shows how important it is for those of the highest rank in society to disapprove of what could destroy another's reputation" (IX, 297).

She herself was assuredly never guilty of this offense, and it is a pity because her portraits could otherwise have been much stronger and have had more bite. Another example, however, in which she does display a more incisive technique is the portrait of Lucrèce's husband Collatin. It could, in fact, be considered a model for this particular genre, and Mlle de Scudéry herself was pleased enough with it to have used it again in one of the volumes of her *Conversations*.

Collatin's physical appearance is neither strikingly good nor is it bad. He is neither intelligent nor is he stupid, and his speech is neither admirably good nor is it excessively bad. He is not without some good sense, but he also is incapable of a precise understanding of things. If he is not at all guilty of having any vice worth mentioning, he also does not have any virtues that could distinguish him from any other man, and if he has not been guilty of cowardice, he also has not given any indication of great courage. Finally, he is one of those men who never says anything that has not already been said, is never blamed or praised for anything he has done, and who during his whole life is spoken of only in reference to someone else. It is often easier to refer to him as the husband of a certain woman or the father of a certain man than to mention his name. (III, 467)

As in her other novels, Mlle de Scudéry gives a great deal of importance to the portrait of the villainous woman of the story, and in this case it is Tullie, the daughter of King Servius Tullius. She is known historically for having run her chariot over her father's corpse (Livy, I, 48).[16] Starting with just this bit of information, Mlle de Scudéry has created in Tullie another grandiose personification of evil.

Mlle de Scudéry, however, has depicted not one but two Tullies. Servius Tullius has two daughters, one symbolizing good, the other evil. The good Tullie is charming, "although of dark complexion," and everyone calls her *La Princesse*. She is gentle and without ambition. Her sister is completely the opposite: "She was tall, blonde, and even rather pretty, but it was a beauty tinged with haughtiness, and she looked more like a hero than a heroine. One could say that she was pretty without being attractive. Her manner was bold, her movements agitated, her voice loud, her spirit domineering, her soul ambitious, and she was so disposed not to give in to anyone that from the time of her early childhood she inspired fear in her sister . . ." (II, 862–63).

The fact that she was a woman disturbed her greatly, as it hindered her in her plans: "I would, without a doubt, rather be a simple soldier than be a woman, because to be truthful, a soldier can become king, but a woman can never become free" (I, 877). Even though she loves Tarquin the superb, whose personality was much like hers, Tullie agrees to marry Prince d'Amériole, since love is secondary in her life. She also thinks that she would be better able to manipulate the prince than she would the domineering Tarquin. "I would be the master of his spirit, either for love or for fear, and then I would make him do as I wish" (II, 896–97).

Tullie then marries the prince, and at the same time Tarquin marries *La Princesse*. Servius Tullius wants these marriages in order to attempt to counterbalance Tullie's violence with her husband's gentleness and to do the same in the case of Tarquin and *La Princesse*. The attraction that Tullie and Tarquin have for each other does not stop with their respective marriages, but Tullie continues to place ambition above everything else: "Although Tullie was incapable of having scruples concerning religion or virtue, she would not allow Tarquin to possess her unless they were married. She feared that if she gratified his desires he would seek other ways to satisfy his ambition and thus hers would be unsatisfied. Only because she wanted to use Tarquin's passions to help her ambitious plans was she so severe in this matter" (II, 955–56).

They finally decide to rid themselves of their respective spouses by assassinating them. Tullie places poison in her husband's bath, and he is overcome by toxic fumes that leave no trace. The poor man takes his time in dying, and Tullie impatiently visits his room from time to time to observe the progress of his death throes. At last "her impatience at the slowness of his dying forced her to strangle him with two of her veils tied together in such a way as to leave no mark of a violent death" (II, 972–73).

Once rid of her husband, Tullie marries Tarquin at last. They are very happy together, and Tarquin now plots to take the throne from Servius Tullius. He proceeds to enjoy clandestine politics so much that he eventually forgets the purpose of it all. When it becomes evident that Servius Tullius does not want Tarquin as a successor, Tullie convinces her husband to rebel and assassinate her own father:

> If you begin, starting from tomorrow, to take the first steps toward mounting the throne, and if you do this with firm resolve and do not turn back from it, I will keep you for my husband and king. But at the same time I want you to know that if you have feelings that are less grand or less ambitious, I consider you a slave and a criminal slave, at that. Because finally, Tarquin, I believe that one is guilty only when committing useless crimes. If we do not mount the throne, then we can be blamed for the death of two persons whom we have sacrificed for our love and our ambition. I am equally persuaded that any crime can be justified if followed by great success. (II, 995–96)

Tarquin is now induced by Tullie's Machiavellianism to dethrone Servius Tullius, and he has the unfortunate king assassinated. Tullie, impatient as ever, cannot wait to know the result of the coup d'état and goes to the senate in her coach. On the way back she finds her father's body lying in the road. Her coachman wants to take another route, but Tullie prevents him from doing so and declares: "Do not stop. There is no road to the throne that is not beautiful!" The horses avoid trodding on the body, but the wheels of the coach succeed in crushing it. As they continue on their way Tullie "turns her head to look at the sight with joy" (II, 1017–18).

Her happiness at becoming queen is disturbed when Clélie is taken prisoner by Tarquin. Now that his ambition has been realized he has the time for other sentiments, and he falls madly in love with Clélie. Tullie is not jealous, but she warns Tarquin that he had better not try to replace her with Clélie: "I want you to know that I, who violated all manner of laws to allow you to reign, will know how to prevent you from ever placing above me a woman who should not look upon Tullie except from her knees" (III, 20). The outraged queen has Clélie watched carefully, waiting for the moment to have her killed, but she is unable to carry out these plans because Clélie is so well protected by her suitors. Tullie continues her politics of manipulation and convinces Porsenna of his own son's treachery. At the end of the novel, however, the truth comes out and the righteous are rewarded. Tullie and Tarquin are forced to flee to Cumae where the local tyrant receives them coldly. The villainous pair die there in "abject misery" (X, 1311).

The portrait that Mlle de Scudéry draws of Tullie and her Machiavellian excesses is not without a certain grandeur. She appears to be greater and stronger than any of the male characters, Tarquin included, because he lets himself be carried away by his love for Clélie, while Tullie is not distracted from her ambitions by any sentiment whatsoever.

### E. *Love and La* Carte de Tendre

In her study of love Mlle de Scudéry condemns "brutal love," such as the case of Paris abducting Helen, but she exalts the love that Hector has for Andromache and the happiness of their union (VIII, 1132). There is nothing more beautiful than a true love, tender and faithful, but the difficulty lies in finding "two persons whose minds are open enough, whose hearts are tender enough, and whose souls are constant enough to love each other ardently and forever" (X, 709). Mlle de Scudéry reminds us that a gallant love is not truly innocent if the two persons involved are not free and do not accept the possibility of marriage. They may not ever marry, but the mere possibility of it leads tender sentiments to a point of perfection (VIII, 917).[17] According to the topography of the *Carte de Tendre,* the single most celebrated facet of *Clélie,* marriage leads lovers to the *Mer Dangereuse* and the *Terres Inconnues.* Because of the difficulties of everyday life, it is easy to become "shipwrecked." Mlle de Scudéry and her friends prefer the security of the *Pays de Tendre,* where reason only dominates all feelings. A tender or platonic love creates a situation for lovers in which there is harmony and an absence of complications. The woman should make access to *Tendre* difficult, and a man should be admitted only after having proved his affection, perseverance, and devotion.

The most direct route to *Tendre,* and the least traveled, is to sail up the *Fleuve d'Inclination.* Although it is the fastest way to reach *Tendre,* only a few, quite privileged persons can take this route. Those lovers less fortunate than Pellisson, who won Mlle de Scudéry's *tendresse* quite rapidly, are generally obliged to travel a much more tortuous road. If they pass through little towns such as *Soumission, Petits Soins, Obéissance,* and *Constante Amitié* and arrive at *Tendre-sur-Reconnaissance,* they are loved as a result of gratitude. On the contrary, traveling through *Jolis Vers, Billets Doux, Générosité,* and *Exactitude* takes them to *Tendre-sur-Estime,* where love comes as a result of respect. In both cases the route is not nearly as direct as the one to *Tendre-sur-Inclination,* and there are certain inherent dangers, such as wandering in the direction of *Méchanceté* and *Médisance* or drowning in the *Lac d'Indifférence.*

If a person should arrive, however, at one of the cities of *Tendre,* he will enjoy a serene happiness made up of small, carefully renewed pleasures. He will experience neither the great ecstacies of love nor its great pain, but will find a form of happiness that can last him a lifetime. *La tendresse,* which must be cultivated, plays an important role in occupying a person's mind, and Mlle de Scudéry sees this as being quite important. At one point Amilcar describes the sadness that comes of not being in love, and to offset this he invents imaginary love affairs: "This passion that I create for myself when I have none in reality agreeably occupies my imagination without troubling my heart, and this amorous disposition, which causes me neither great pain nor great joy, allows me a most pleasant reverie" (III, 71). Reverie, as a matter of fact, plays a large role in *"sentiments tendres."* It is a kind of restlessness that causes a lover to walk through the woods musing over his beloved.

As for the woman, she holds a position of preeminence in the kingdom of *Tendre.* If she stays at one of the "safe" cities, she will remain happy, independent, and mistress of her destiny. The situation is quite different, however, if she travels to the *Terres Inconnues* and marries.

Mlle de Scudéry's attitude toward marriage is rather negative, and in the novel few husbands are faithful to their wives. As a matter of fact, she says that "marriage and love are two things that do not often last together" (VIII, 1407). Even admitting that the husband loves his wife before marrying, the situation changes, and if it is a case of an arranged marriage "the familiarity of married life does not encourage love to grow" (VI, 865). There is, in effect, a great difference between love and marriage. "An *honnête homme* must marry for the good of his family but should love as he pleases" (VIII, 1343). Clearly, then, marriage is a business matter, love a private affair.

If a husband does not love his wife, he naturally assumes the role of master, if not tyrant. Widowhood, therefore, is a privileged condition: "In losing a husband one loses a master who is often an obstacle to the enjoyment of many things" (IV, 1025). Needless to say, this is said by a widow who has been quickly consoled. This might explain why so many of Mlle de Scudéry's friends were widows and why they were so reluctant to profit from new opportunities to remarry. Mme de Sévigné is probably the most celebrated example of this situation, so aptly described by Abbé de Pure in *La Prétieuse*, as "this pleasant escape from captivity."[18]

It should not be thought that Mlle de Scudéry was completely against marriage. She was against the kind of marriage that forced a young girl to marry without her consent. One should not forget that Clélie and Aronce marry at the end of the novel, as well as the other heroes and heroines. Marriage, however, is much more successful in fiction, where only idealized characters are involved, than in real life.

The writing of these three epic novels enabled Mlle de Scudéry to make some important contributions. As Sainte-Beuve has pointed out, she performed the function of teacher in her effort to define *politesse* and to propagate the necessary rules for having a pleasant social life. In doing so she depicted a fascinating tableau of the *société précieuse* in which she played so eminent a role, and according to Adam, her works are indispensable for the study of this often misunderstood movement. We can also trace through her books the change that took place in the seventeenth century in regard to a woman's role in society. From a position of preeminence, which is so clearly seen in the heroic novels, women began to react differently in the *nouvelles* as a result of a new way of thinking that characterized the second half of the seventeenth century. Mlle de Scudéry's novels certainly reflected the mentality of the time and had an indisputable charm for her contemporaries. Much of the same charm still awaits the unsuspecting reader of today who has the time and the desire to explore this *terre inconnue*.

## CHAPTER 3

# The Short Stories

MLLE de Scudéry is known, above all, for her epic novels and, perhaps, for the work of her later years, the *Conversations morales*, but her *nouvelles* remain practically unknown. It is particularly interesting to see that she was sensitive to the changes in taste of her contemporaries and that after *Clélie* she stopped writing the long novel to concentrate on the production of *histoires* and *nouvelles*, which became fashionable at the time. René Godenne in his article "Les Nouvelles de Mlle de Scudéry"[1] analyses *Célinte*, *Mathilde d'Aguilar*, and *La Promenade de Versailles*, all of which were published independently. There are, however, other works of varying lengths in the volumes of *Conversations* that equally merit the title of *histoire* or *nouvelle*.

In the second volume of *La Morale du monde*, "L'Histoire de Bélinde" is halfway between being a *nouvelle* and a *conversation*, as is well expressed by its subtitle, "Histoire et conversation d'amitié." At the end of this work, which is about fifty pages long, the interlocutors comment: "I never would have believed that a story about friendship, without stirring adventures, could have been so interesting" (419).[2] "L'Histoire du Prince Ariaméne" appeared in *Les Entretiens de morale* of 1692, and it was the last love story written by Mlle de Scudéry. It is interesting to note that it has a tragic ending.

*Nouvelles* are of various lengths, ranging from about fifty pages to several hundred. They can be, as in the case of *Célanire*, relatively simple in plot, or they can be, on the contrary, extremely complicated, as is the case of *Célinte*. They all have, however, one point in common: conversations about ethics, psychology, or art are dispersed throughout the narratives. Toward the end of her career Mlle de Scudéry gradually dedicated less space to the narratives and concentrated more on conversations. These conversations took on a more personal tone as time went by, and, as a result, they give us a clear picture of some of the author's more characteristic ideas.

### I Célinte, Nouvelle première

This work was published anonymously by Courbé in January of 1661. It is somewhat surprising that it did not appear under the name of Georges de Scudéry, as all of the others did, because he was still alive at the time. Whatever the reason, Mlle de Scudéry, in the preface, refers to her anonymity in this way: "Reader, don't be too curious in seeking the author's name. I am forbidden to tell it to you, but you will be able to guess it easily enough if you only have some knowledge of high society and some acquaintance with the famous works of this sort."

Despite the somewhat arrogant tone of the preface, which is rather unlike Mlle de Scudéry's usual manner, her authorship of this work has never been in question. The many passages borrowed from *Clélie* and the fact that Bosquillon formally attributed the book to Mlle de Scudéry explain why bibliographers have never seriously doubted her authorship of this work. It can be remembered that although all her books after *Célinte* were published anonymously, there was no doubt as to the identity of their author.

The first eighty pages of *Célinte* are occupied with a conversation of a group assembled at a property owned by Cléonime, which, according to Chatelain, was a depiction of Fouquet's mansion at Saint-Mandé.[3] This conversation deals with curiosity and the various forms it could take. Mlle de Scudéry reutilized a part of a conversation from *Clélie* that spoke of people who had the ability to open letters not meant for their eyes, read them, and then seal them without anyone being aware of it. She condemned this practice once again, commenting that: "It is as bad a habit as looking at someone else's hand while playing cards" (54). Curiosity could also cause one to want to know the future, and this could lead to the study of astrology, of which Mlle de Scudéry disapproved. She equally criticized those curious to see famous people or places, because their curiosity was not inspired by a true interest but merely by a desire to be able to speak about them. She then took aim at the people who collect things. She scorned those who collected "butterflies, caterpillars, spiders," but not those whose interest was in paintings or statues (72–77). Here one can see, perhaps, a barb directed at Georges de Scudéry who, besides his collection of paintings, also had a variety of odd objects, and who once spent a large sum of money to acquire a collection of tulips.[4]

Curiosity, however, could have its good side, such as creating in Artélice a desire to read a *nouvelle* that had been placed at her disposal just before leaving Paris. Now the group has gathered at the mansion, and all will listen to a reading of this *nouvelle*. Its setting remains somewhat vague, but it has to do with a contemporary tale: "In order not to deceive the reader, I advise him that all of the names in the *nouvelle* are fictitious, but there is evidence to show that the story took place in our century, and at one of the most beautiful courts of Europe" (80).

Célinte is a young orphan who is raised by her aunt. She is courted by two worthy young men, Méliandre and Ariston, but she loves neither one of them. Attraction to another person is difficult to explain, and worthiness is not the only cause: "Attraction is the result of a profound and secret judgement that affects us without our immediate knowledge, rather than being, as many believe, a feeling deprived of all reason" (118). A certain amount of mystery, therefore, is a part of the development of "this sweet folly that cannot do without melancholy" (159). This is one of Mlle de Scudéry's often repeated ideas: melancholy is necessarily linked with love.

When Poliante arrives on the scene, Célinte falls in love with him, but he does not return this love until later, and this angers Célinte because she does not like being the first to love. She fears that what Poliante feels for her is only an *amour de reconnaissance*, and that she could not be happy with it. She then expresses the power of love in these words which emphasize the intensity of this feeling: "It is not necessary to know why one loves in order to love well. It is not necessary at all to say 'I love because I am loved' . . . but only to say 'I love because I love, because I can do nothing else but love, because I cannot stop myself from loving' " (195).

Célinte and Poliante are married, but immediately after the ceremony Poliante is arrested because he has been politically compromised. Méliante, who is very much in favor with the prince, hopes to be able to have the marriage between Célinte and Poliante annulled, "because, after all, she was not his wife" (221). Here he is referring to the fact that the marriage had not yet been consummated. Faced with this dangerous situation, and fearing for Poliante's life, Célinte decides to pass for dead. She leaves for the country, has her death announced, and finds refuge in a convent. Poliante escapes from prison in order to pray at the tomb of his beloved Célinte, unaware that her death is only a ruse. He then flees to another country, and soon word comes that he, too, is dead. Later, Poliante returns and has the opportunity during a battle to demonstrate his valor. He wins back the respect of the king and finds his Célinte alive. Their joyous reunion brings the narrative to a close.

This rather complicated story is remarkable for its macabre aspects, something rarely found in Mlle de Scudéry's works. During a large part of the narrative the author relates the suffering of the newlyweds. Célinte, believing that Poliante is dead, desires to end her own life, and he, too, desperately seeks death because of having lost the woman he loved. Poliante secretly visits Célinte's supposed tomb and finds it empty (254). Célinte obtains a coffin containing an embalmed body which is not, to be sure, that of Poliante (270). Mixed in with these extraordinary incidents there is a moralistic pattern which clearly says: Even that which is destined for amusement is of higher value "with some trace of ethics ingeniously placed" (384). Mlle de Scudéry's commentary on this tale is not lacking in irony. She points out that a love of this type was not a usual one in her century. In fact, "far from loving suitors or husbands when one believes them to be dead, one forgets them even while they are in sight, and even to the point of forgetting that they even existed" (380).

## II  Mathilde

### A. *Les Jeux*

The original edition of 1667 was published anonymously and did not carry the subtitle that was added to the 1704 edition: "Spanish and French Story, true and gallant, written by M. D. S." It was published again at The Hague in 1736, and there was a pirated edition in 1756, attributed to Mme de V., which came out under the title of *Anecdotes of the Court of Alphonse XI, King of Castile.*[5]

As in *Célinte*, there are two totally different parts, each having its own title. The first part, entitled *"Les Jeux servant de préface à Mathilde"* ("The games which serve as a preface to *Mathilde*"), comprises 128 pages. The second part is the actual story of Mathilde d'Aguilar, and it is 518 pages in length. The preface, or first part,

gives a picture of the *Précieux* and their pastimes. A group consist-
ing of five women and four men leaves Paris by carriage for a house
in the country, situated on the banks of the Seine. The company is
pleasant and the rules of the trip dictate that its purpose shall be to
amuse oneself. The travelers decide to give themselves fictitious
names and select some found in *Cyrus* and *Clélie*.

They begin to discuss the pleasures of life, and Plotine, reacting
in accordance with the joyful nature of this character in *Clélie*,
defends all pleasures, even "little games." She expresses herself in
this manner: "When a rather large group of people get together and
a certain spirit of joy reigns supreme, and, not wanting to take a
walk or to speak of serious matters one simply wishes to dally in an
amusing way, I do not disapprove at all of little games, as long as one
takes them for what they are" (26). Herminius, Pellisson's namesake
in *Clélie*, is stubborn and inflexible as is his wont and responds: "If
one takes them for what they are, one takes them for mere trifles
that should not occupy the time of reasonable people" (26).

The dispute continues and revolves around the usefulness of the
games. At last their origin is discussed, and it is agreed upon that
they were invented in Lydia during a famine where they were
needed to distract people from their hunger. Now they themselves,
in order to pass the time, begin to play a game often mentioned in
novels, and which was popular in the salons of the *Précieuses*. They
all write extremely varied tasks on identical square pieces of paper.
Then each draws a piece of paper and must do whatever is ordered.

Plotine is the first to try, and her task is to explain why a handsome fool is more foolish than any other (40). Philiste must make a
comparison between a flatterer and one who is always obliging (44).
Some of the tasks are much more complex in nature, such as to
compose an elegy or a madrigal, or to give a detailed description of a
house in the country. This particular subject leads to a description of
the *Palais de Saint-Cloud*, which belongs to *Monsieur*, the king's
brother, to whom *Mathilde* is dedicated. In passing, Mlle de Scudéry pays discrete homage to Mme de Lafayette, who has already
begun to work on *Madame*'s biography, known today as *La Vie de la
Princesse d'Angleterre*.[6] She refrains from giving a detailed portrait
of *Madame*, explaining: "I wouldn't think of portraying her, knowing
that there already is a description that resembles her much better
than I could hope to do here" (111).

The last to draw her assignment is Noromate. She must relate a
story and is delighted to do so because a friend, just before her

departure, had given her an interesting manuscript. She reads it to her friends the following day because they are now about to attend a superb feast hosted by *Monsieur* and *Madame*, to which all of the nobility of the area are invited. The story that Noromate reads is *Mathilde*.

## B. *The Story*

The author indicates on the first page that the goal of the book is, as usual, to instruct and to divert. The story takes place in two settings, one in Castile and one in Avignon, at the time when the popes had their residence there. The historical basis is a serious one, and the author is precise in explaining the history of fourteenth century Castile. Strangely enough the king is called Alphonse XIII, which is, of course, incorrect. In reality it is a reference to Alphonse XI, king of Castile, and son of Ferdinand IV. It also mentions the king's mistress, Leonora de Guzman, and his son, the future Pedro the Cruel, who poisoned his wife Blanche of Bourbon. Even though no precise date is mentioned during the story, the action takes place around 1341, when Petrarch received the laurel crown in Rome.

King Alphonse thinks of marrying the beautiful Constance, but the marriage does not materialize, and the disappointed woman, who had hoped to be queen, is obliged to marry Rodolphe d'Aguilar. Because of political struggles, Constance, her husband, and their little daughter, Mathilde, leave in exile. They travel to Avignon, where the pope's court is unique for its "gallantry and civility." Among the many elegant and beautiful personages "there was one girl celebrated for her beauty, her wit, and her virtue, whose name was known throughout the world for the extreme love the famous Petrarch had for her" (10).

The personages of Laura and Petrarch are represented as the prototypes of the love that exists at *Tendre*. Here historical facts are ignored, and there is absolutely no mention of Laura's husband and their eleven children. She is depicted as a young girl who loves Petrarch, but who cannot marry him because of financial problems. Both see each other constantly and are content to share a spiritual love.

The moment Laura sees Mathilde she forms a friendship with her, and Petrarch shapes her intellect and teaches her Provençal and Italian. Mlle de Scudéry obviously remembered her stay in this region and her visit to the monastery where some relics associated with Laura were kept. She also had not forgotten the Provençal language and speaks of its grandeur: "It was known everywhere, having had as representatives some of the most ingenious poets that the greatest of Italians were not ashamed to imitate, and whose works could still be found in manuscript form throughout the principal cities of the kingdom" (17). Once again Mlle de Scudéry is utilizing the memories of her travels and her own personal knowledge. When she quotes Petrarch in Italian she is demonstrating her mastery of the language and her love of commenting on his sonnets, as Mme de Sévigné has pointed out in a letter to Mme de Grignan.[7]

Avignon, at that time, was one of the intellectual centers of Europe, and Mathilde, maturing in this milieu, acquires its tastes and principles. She does not want to marry, and wants, instead, to have a life like that enjoyed by Petrarch and Laura. Unfortunately, the happiness of the three friends is short-lived because Petrarch leaves for Rome to receive his laurel crown, and Mathilde must return to Castile with her father, who has made a political agreement with the king. Mathilde's mother, Constance, is so angered by the turn of events that she dies.

Once again in Spain, Mathilde lives at court and has a great deal of success. Her father pursues his political ambitions and forms an alliance with Don Albert de Benavidez. In order to solidify the alliance the two men wish to have their respective children marry. Mathilde is very unhappy because she does not want to marry, but, on the other hand, she wants to stay in society and is not at all attracted by the veil, the only alternative for a young girl who disobeys her father. Fortunately, Don Alphonse de Benavidez, who has received an excellent education "that permits him to make up his own mind" (195), has decided to dedicate himself to the pursuit of glory, so that he, too, has chosen not to marry. Without actually meeting, the two young people agree, through letters, not to outwardly oppose their fathers' wishes, but to provoke certain delays that prevent the realization of the matrimonial plans. Mathilde sums up their attitudes in this way: "I love freedom as much as he loves glory, and I am as much inclined toward tranquillity as he is toward ambition" (109).

The two fathers, however, discover the truth, and Alphonse must flee in order to avoid the consequences of their anger. He leaves without ever having seen Mathilde, who, by the grace of her own father's death is "in full possession of her liberty and . . . leads the sweetest and most pleasant life imaginable" (122). After having covered himself with glory as a soldier, Alphonse returns to Castile and finally encounters Mathilde at a bullfight. When he learns exactly who she is, he begins to regret his past attitude. He still wishes no part of marriage, but "the thought of having refused the possession of such a one as Mathilde makes him very unhappy" (150). Little by little, as the two young people become better acquainted, they admit that they love each other. Mathilde, however, wishes to impose on Alphonse the type of relationship that was shared by Petrarch and Laura. This does not please Alphonse at all, who desires much more: "Alphonse was extremely disappointed with the apparent impossibility of ever possessing Mathilde, especially after having had the opportunity to marry her. The thought caused him many unhappy hours" (270).

Naturally Mathilde has other suitors, among which is the prince, Don Pedro. Although he tries in vain to abduct Mathilde, he does succeed in having Alphonse leave again for the wars. This saddens Mathilde, who now reflects on the pain caused by love, and even by friendship: "I assure you that if one sought only peace, one would avoid both love and friendship, indifference being a refuge from the most painful misfortunes of life" (349).

Alphonse returns to court once again having gloriously defeated the Moors, and hopes that the king will give him Mathilde's hand as recompense for his exploits. Alphonse XI, however, after so many years, still regrets not having married Constance, and now wants to marry her daughter. Mathilde refuses his offer, saying: "I don't dream at all of marrying. I have no ambition other than that of dying free." The king responds in a manner not without a certain *grandeur cornélienne*: "But my child, to be queen is to be free!" (446). Mathilde later explains her strong attachment for freedom and her refusal to marry the young Alphonse: "I have, for him, some respect, some gratitude, and, if I dare say, some affection, but I have been unable to renounce my freedom in his favor" (456).

The king is jealous of Alphonse and imprisons him, but while there the young man overhears plans for an attempt to free the king of the Moors, who is in a nearby cell. Ever faithful to his king, Alphonse divulges what he knows, and succeeds in wrecking the plot. Alphonse XI now gives thought to the young man's grandeur and to his own mediocrity. He proves victorious over himself and grants Mathilde's hand to Alphonse. Her reason for accepting the situation is an interesting one. She marries Alphonse because she has given such proof of her passion for him that only by marriage can she dispel any doubt concerning her innocence. Without this she probably would have wanted to continue their platonic relationship, which weighed so heavily on the young man.

Mathilde abandons, then, her independence for Alphonse, who, in turn, abandons his ambition for her sake. He is sent as ambassador to Avignon, where the happy couple will live the rest of their lives. Their marriage is a good one: "Mathilde and Alphonse find in their alliance all that could make them happy. They desire no more than what they have. They both love each other without jealousy" (516), and they have "found the way to be free despite being married" (508). Here marriage is placed on the same pedestal as the *tendre amitié* that unites Petrarch and Laura and Mlle de Scudéry makes this comment: "These four persons have furnished a model for perfect love in two different ways" (517).

## C. *The value of this* Nouvelle

Although *Mathilde* retains certain elements of the heroic novel— such as the fire started by Pedro as a diversionary measure in his attempt to abduct Mathilde, the long description of the siege of Tarisse, the duels, and the punishment of the evil personages at the end—the *nouvelle*'s principal value lies in its psychological analysis.

The character of Mathilde is well constructed. Raised in an unusual manner, she has developed her own ideas and wants to apply them while maintaining her freedom. Love gradually breaks down the barriers she has raised, and marriage eventually fulfills the desires clearly expressed by Alphonse. He is not the chivalrous hero who is content to be in a woman's thrall. He is a young man who, at first, is ambitious and insensitive to love, and then, little by little, is detached from his search for glory by the love he increasingly feels for Mathilde.

The psychological concept of these two characters is different from that of those found in epic novels, and is much closer in taste to the modern reader. The other characters, such as Laura and Petrarch, are somewhat superficial in nature. This is, curiously, the opposite situation from the epic novels in which the principal characters—such as Ibrahim, Mandane, Aronce and Clélie—are depicted conventionally, while the secondary personages—such as *Le Marquis français* in *Ibrahim,* and Plotine, Amilcar or Bérélise in *Clélie*—are portrayed in a more realistic manner. *Mathilde d'Agui-*

*lar* retains, however, one of the most successful elements of the epic novel, and that is the inclusion of conversations that cover a wide variety of subjects. This mixture of the old and the new has resulted in some of Mlle de Scudéry's most attractive material for the contemporary reader.

### III La Promenade de Versailles

#### A. *Structure*

Published in 1669, this work has been called a novel by M. Ratner.[8] Even though it does, in fact, have the proportions of a novel, being close to seven hundred pages in length, it belongs, however, to the same genre as *Mathilde*. It, too, combines a contemporary story with conversations on numerous and various subjects.

The first hundred pages are dedicated to a long introduction in which a group of friends meet at Versailles in the company of a beautiful foreigner who speaks perfect French. They converse while visiting the castle and its gardens, still in an unfinished state. Mlle de Scudéry gives a precise description of the area, one that has been often quoted in studies of Versailles, and this also adds an historical value to the work.[9]

The second part of the book concerns "The Story of Célanire" the young, beautiful foreigner. She is in the company of Glicère, a relative, who relates the details that led to the young woman's exile, and tells of her love for Cléandre. Then Cléandre himself arrives to continue the tale, and describes the events that have taken place since Célanire's departure. The "Histoire de Célanire," therefore, is composed of two parts: one a lengthy account of Célanire's past, of which she is aware, and the other a short narrative coming at the end of the *nouvelle* in which she learns, along with the others, what has happened since her flight. All of this is intermingled with numerous discussions and conversations of great interest.

#### B. *The Story*

As in *Célinte*, Mlle de Scudéry assures the reader that the story is a true one: "Ordinarily novels utilize famous names that serve as a foundation for fictitious events, but here the adventures are true and the names are fictitious" (104). The story unfolds in a court of which little is known except that it strongly resembles the French

court. Mlle de Scudéry takes great care to explain why the principal
characters know the French language and culture so well, considering that they are foreigners. Cléandre lived in France, where he
learned the language. Célanire studied it as a child, and Glicère's
mother, who is now living in this foreign court, is French. The three
women often meet to speak the language together.

Célanire is, as are many of Mlle de Scudéry's heroines, an orphan, and is raised by her uncle. He allows her a great deal of
freedom, and she lives happily at the court of the ruling sovereign,
who is referred to as the "prince." The only limitation imposed on
Célanire is that she not marry Cléandre, a man quite accomplished,
but belonging to a family her uncle detests. Naturally it is with him
that she falls in love. Cléandre loves her too, and the two of them
are careful to keep their love a secret.

The uncle, however, always suspicious, wants to force his niece to
marry. He schemes to have as fiancé Cléonte, the richest man of the
court, but also the least attractive, physically and intellectually. In
order to escape from her uncle, Célanire enters a convent, but she
learns that he wants to abduct her and force her to submit to his will.
She then goes into exile with Glicère, while Cléandre, who has
killed a rival in a duel, leaves the country to join a foreign army. On
the way he is kidnapped by pirates, and Célanire languishes in the
thought that she is in a strange country without news of her beloved,
whom she believes to be enslaved. He is, instead, demonstrating his
prowess in a series of remarkable adventures.

While Célanire is visiting the castle of Versailles, Cléandre arrives to relate the story of his escape. He was able to lead the slaves
in a revolt against the Turks and thereby gain his own freedom. As if
this were not enough, he also tells of regaining the prince's favor by
rendering him a great political service, and of having saved Célanire's uncle from death, thus causing him to consent to their
marriage.

Besides Cléandre and Célanire, there is another couple that is of
some interest—the prince and his fiancée, Argélinde. She loves the
prince, but he does not feel the same for her. Since she is aware of
this, she is jealous of everyone, especially Célanire, whom she considers to be the woman most capable of seducing the prince. In fact,
he is quite sensitive to Célanire's charm, but, unlike Suleiman in
*Ibrahim*, he is able to control his feelings because he knows that the

young girl loves, and is loved by, Cléandre. He decides never to love again, and marries Argélinde off to a prince of another country far away.

## C. *The Conversations*

As in all of Mlle de Scudéry's works there is the usual discussion of love. Célanire does not want to love: "I am resolved to do whatever I can never to love anyone, and . . . if I did allow myself to be loved, I would never choose you." She says this to Cléandre, making an allusion to the fact that their families were enemies. On the other hand, he is favored by the prince and gives a great deal of time to affairs of state. Célanire sees in this, too, another factor that would impede their love from being durable and happy: "You are too much at Court to be capable of a constant love, and I find fleeting romances to be totally worthless" (178–79). Célanire tries to stifle the feelings she has for Cléandre because she feels, as the princesse de Clèves does later, an attraction for "renunciation." "Let us eliminate this feeling. Let us love no one in all of our lives, and let us live without pleasure and without pain" (230). She fears, in effect, that she will be less loved once married: "Because of the way my heart is made I would die if after having become your wife you came to love me no longer" (200). Cléandre is more fortunate, however, than M. de Nemours, and he is able to convince Célanire of the seriousness of his passion.

Love is not the only subject dealt with by Mlle de Scudéry in this work. She also touches on literature and politics. At the beginning of the book some of the conversations are in regard to the usefulness of descriptions in novels. Télamon sees in them "the delight of the imagination," while Glicère "passes over them and seeks the heroes as if she herself were a part of their adventures and a rival to the heroines" (5). Mlle de Scudéry supported the need for descriptions, expecially for the purpose of conserving the memory of things that might one day be destroyed. She also saw description as an aid to comprehension: "It is certain that in order to understand well the events that take place, it is necessary for the mind to have a clear conception of the places where these events happen, and it is for this reason that geography, which is no more than a general description of the world, is doubtlessly needed for an understanding of history" (9).

*and politica?*

The mention of history diverts the conversation to a subject dear to Mlle de Scudéry, and that is history's connection with the novel. "Novels are a type of poetry, but they are more closely tied to history, and whereas in poems one can express things that go beyond plausibility, the well-made novel is obliged to follow the rules of authenticity" (18–19). It may be noted that even during the period of her epic novels Mlle de Scudéry preached the necessity to respect plausibility, even though, for the modern reader, she did not always strictly practice what she preached.

The tone of *La Promenade de Versailles* is sometimes rather personal, and Mlle de Scudéry allows us some insight into her opinions regarding literature. She expresses her lack of inclination toward the works of Voiture, in which a superficial type of love plays a greater role than that of *tendresse* (203). She also voices some reservations in regard to La Rochefoucauld, whose works contain, for her, too much pessimism, but in which she admires his sense of psychological analysis. His book, *Maximes et réflexions*, gives us the thoughts of a "man of high birth and great merit who has, in some way, dissected the hearts of all men and has even discovered stains on the purest of virtues" (132).

A large part of the conversations is given to the praise of Louis XIV. One of his roles in the artistic realm was to establish academies "with the purpose of surpassing the knowledge of the ancients and perfecting all sciences and arts" (94). The palace that he was having constructed, with its superb gardens and fountains, illustrated his glory. Another manifestation was the magnificent *fêtes* that he was giving. Mlle de Scudéry mentions the *Grand Divertissement royal* of 1668 to celebrate the peace of Aix-la-Chapelle, at which time a "pleasant comedy of Molière was presented" (586). She was referring to *Georges Dandin*, given with interludes and concluding with a ballet comprised of one hundred dancers. The comedy we see today, without the interludes and the ballet, no longer resembles the entertainment Mlle de Scudéry had enjoyed. In passing one can note that if she had harbored any ill feelings toward Molière because of *Les Précieuses ridicules*, she could have omitted mentioning his name as she did in the case of Lully, who composed the music for the production.

The praise for the king inspires a discussion of a political order on the respective values of different types of government. Mlle de Scudéry is convinced of the superiority of an hereditary monarchy.

"A hundred times I have considered in astonishment that men who have established so many different kinds of government have never succeeded so well as when they give up their own wisdom to rely upon that of a higher order. Never have they encountered the grandeur, tranquillity, and durability of state as when they choose their ruler from one family, father to son, accepting whom God has chosen for them" (n.p.).

Mlle de Scudéry once again is expressing her loyalty to the royal family, and her confidence in the order established by the divine architect who governs the universe. Being a friend of Leibnitz, she often found the opportunity to repeat this belief. Her approval of the king does not, however, extend to his courtiers, whom she mocks through the remarks made by the hermit Philémon, at court against his will. He makes a commentary that La Rochefoucauld would not have disavowed: "Very often men don't know at all where their happiness lies, and they spend their lives either desiring what they don't have or regretting what they no longer have, although when they had it they were not aware of its value" (145). Philémon has painted a strongly negative picture of courtiers, but it is in verbal form and said to a friend. Mlle de Scudéry accepts this type of mockery, which is general and not widely publicized. She detests, however, the *"misérable satirique,"* who attacks a person in such a way as to leave no doubt as to his identity.

In the *nouvelle* there is mention of such a satirist who has used Célanire as a subject for his vicious pen. Her friends discuss the manner in which they should react to this. Cléandre contends that "it is necessary to scorn such behavior but not to show any anger because silence is the best rebuke that can be given in such affairs" (338). Since, however, Cléandre is in a position of power and does not want to let this offense go unpunished, he is able to have the satirist arrested and placed in prison. Can we see in this, then, a vengeance on the part of Mlle de Scudéry upon the brothers Boileau, intellectual though it may be?

## IV "Les Bains des Thermopyles"

This text of about two hundred pages is part of Volume II of the *Conversations sur divers sujets* and was published in 1680. Although it is announced as a journal written for the princess of Milet, it is actually a *nouvelle*. The story takes place at the foot of a mountain

range "that divides Greece in two" (Cyrus, X, 584). Mlle de Scudéry
reuses here her description found in Volume IX of *Cyrus* which
contains the story of Pisistrate. According to Victor Cousin[10] this
was a depiction of Le Canigou in the Pyrenees. The setting is the
same, but the story told here is not found in *Cyrus*.

Mlle de Scudéry gives us a picture of a spa as it was in the
seventeenth century. One can note the change in the concept of
decency between the spa that Montaigne described in his *Journal de
Voyage en Italie*,[11] a spa in which men and women bathed together,
and the one that Mlle de Scudéry depicts. She shows us the men
and women separated by a balustrade where guards keep a steady
surveillance. To insure even more privacy, the men bathe in the
morning and the women in the evening. Mlle de Scudéry has
doubts as to the therapeutic benefits of the baths, but she does value
the tranquillity one derives from them, and "this can have only a
favorable effect on one's health and beauty" (622).

The story takes place during the fifth century B.C., and Mlle de
Scudéry once again demonstrates her knowledge of ancient Greek
history and literature. She makes allusions to great historical events
and, in passing, mentions Alcibiades, Socrates, Xenophon, etc. Using
casual references, she is able to establish the setting she desires for
her story. For example, some returning soldiers come to thank
Euripides for being the cause of their liberation. Taken prisoner
during the expedition to Sicily, they recited some choruses from
*The Phoenissae* for the Sicilian prince, who granted them their freedom because "he did not want to keep as prisoners people who had
such beautiful thoughts in their minds" (703). This reference to such
a well-known event sets the period in which the story is supposed to
take place, even though the style of life described is clearly that of
the seventeenth century. Whereas *Célinte* and *La Promenade de
Versailles* take place in an epoch contemporary to their publication,
with "Les Bains des Thermopyles" Mlle de Scudéry returns to the
style of the epic novel, which utilizes a celebrated period in history.

The story, which is extremely simple, is about Mélicrite and
Théramène, whose political role is not at all analysed here.
Théramène loves the young girl, and she is not insensitive to his
passion,but she is afraid of the future: "She was generally persuaded
that there was no man capable of loving only one woman in all of his
life, and she did not want to expose herself to being no longer loved
or loved less than before" (646). She preferred to marry an "honest

man" whom she did not love, rather than be neglected by a man she did love: "When I think of what my pain should be to see him have for another woman the same tenderness he had for me, I reconfirm my resolution never to marry anyone, and nothing can change this" (652).

Despite this declaration, Mélicrite lets herself gradually respond to Théramène's attentions. When Athens is ravaged by the plague, Théramène nurses Mélicrite's father back to health, and the grateful man offers his daughter's hand in marriage as a reward (680). Théramène refuses on the grounds that Mélicrite, herself, must willingly consent to the marriage. Just as the last of her reluctance is about to melt, a decree is announced that obliges Athenians to take two wives in order to repopulate the city decimated by disease and war.[12]

Mélicrite, embittered by this, flees to the *vierges voilées* (an anachronistic counterpart to the seventeenth century nunnery), but the high priestess refuses to admit her. She explains why in this interesting comment: "When one leaves the world to serve the gods, one should not be as vexed as you are. It is necessary to have a tranquil spirit and be free to reason clearly. When one comes among the veiled virgins she must not have a heart filled with conflicting passions. One must leave the world only when she is not angry with it" (807).

In order to calm Mélicrite's fears, Théramène officially swears that he will not follow the decree. If to marry her means to live in exile he is ready to do so. This is not necessary, however, as they learn that the decree is not mandatory but only means that a man has permission to take a second wife. Théramène then weds Mélicrite, and Mlle de Scudéry foresees a happy married life for them because: "Love and marriage are rarely found together, and it is this rarity that will ensure the happiness of Théramène and Mélicrite" (832).

Published two years after *La Princesse de Clèves*, this text presents itself as a variation on the theme of "refusal" so brilliantly developed by Mme de Lafayette. Mlle de Scudéry, however, is more optimistic in her approach, and if marriages are not always happy, love can surely bring about happiness, as is almost entirely the case in her novels.

One can also see, in a long conversation on the fear of death and sickness, an allusion to a contemporary situation. Mme de Sablé, to whom Mlle de Scudéry was rather close, had just died in 1678. It is possible to see in the description of Eupolie, who lived in terror of sickness and death, a direct reference to Mme de Sablé and her well-known weakness. At one point, Eupolie declares: "If I were as beautiful as Venus, and someone offered to bring me back to life after I died, but I had to come back ugly, old, and unhappy, I would take him at his word, because I would rather be horribly ugly, old, and unhappy and live, than be dead" (762). This seems to be an allusion to Montaigne's *Les Essais*[13], but Mlle de Scudéry went on to advocate, just as Montaigne did, the necessity to prepare for one's death: "I think about death when the occasion arises, but I think of it without fear, because one day, without fail, I will see it closer than I do now, and I think it best that we are not total strangers" (767–68).

### V   "L'Histoire du Comte d'Albe"

A. *The Story*

The last four hundred pages of the *Conversations nouvelles sur divers sujets*, published in 1684, are dedicated to the "Histoire du Comte d'Albe." The usual format is used, in which a group of friends gather to discuss a certain subject. This time the subject is glory, and someone reads the story of the Comte d'Albe. Mlle de Scudéry cites her sources of information with great precision: "The actual basis for this story can be found in the history of the joining together of Portugal and Castile, page 206, in the translation published by Bilaine in 1680" (594). In reality Mlle de Scudéry notably modified the actual historical facts.

This story takes place in Spain during the sixteenth century at the court of Philipe II. Mlle de Scudéry is aware that she is depicting French customs that certainly could not be applied to the Spanish court of that time, especially in regard to the freedom of women. She takes the trouble to explain, however, that family alliances allow the young people to see each other "with more freedom than is usual in Spain" (605).

The comte is a very attractive young man and his father fears that he will fall in love with the beautiful Théodore. She has many fine qualities but her father has gone into exile for political reasons, and the Duc d'Albe wants for his son a marriage that will strengthen their position at the court. Théodore and the comte love each other nevertheless, and they correspond regularly. The comte, however, writes the name of another young girl, Jacinte, on the letter in order not to arouse his father's suspicion if one were to be lost. This excess of precaution nearly leads to disaster for the young people. Jacinte really loves the comte and will stop at nothing to get what she wants. She bribes one of the comte's servants to bring her all of the letters exchanged by the two lovers, and is able to open and reseal them without leaving any evidence. When Théodore is forced to go into exile as a result of an accusation that she has pro-French leanings, the comte sends her a letter in which he proposes marriage. Naturally he has addressed it to Jacinte, and when it comes into her possession she uses it to attempt to force the unhappy young man to marry her. The comte must now reveal the truth to his father. Despite the Duc d'Albe's reputation for ferocity, he reacts in a paternal fashion and allows his son to marry Théodore in secret. The queen, who is fond of Jacinte, is angry because she believes the letter to be truly addressed to the young girl and fears that dishonor would come to her if a man as respected as the Comte d'Albe now refused to keep his word without reason. Since the comte is absent from the court, the queen has the Duc d'Albe arrested. When his son hears of this he rushes to the court to free his father, and at the same time Jacinte tries in vain to poison Théodore, who is at a convent awaiting the return of her husband.

The complicated situation is cleared up with the arrival of the servant who has been giving the Comte d'Albe's letters to Jacinte. His testimony entirely exonerates the young man, and the father and son are further aided by the imminent war with Portugal which will make their services necessary. The king, then, is disposed to forget the secret intrigues and the fact that the son of one of his favorites had married a girl in exile for political reasons.

## B. *Description of French Poetry in the XVIth Century*

A group of Théodore's friends greatly admire French culture, which explains the accusation that sends her into exile, and it furnishes the subject for many of their discussions. A French nobleman, who is related to the poet Mellin de Saint-Gelais, is present at one of the discussions in which they will listen to a letter that describes the state of contemporary French literature. The hostess has authorized the reading of the letter with these conditions: "I consent to it if I can ask questions whenever I please and if conversation can be mixed in with the reading, because I swear to you that long readings overwhelm me. I am also often quite angry reading even the best of books because they cannot respond to the objections that come to my mind" (41).[14] Everyone agrees to interrupt the reading with questions and commentaries, and, in fact, they eagerly comply with her wishes. The Frenchman, who knows all of the writers mentioned either personally or by reputation, offers to satisfy the curiosity of the listeners. It can be safely assumed that here we have a description of one of the literary meetings of the *Précieuses*.

It is particularly interesting to note that in the introduction to his edition of *Le Tableau de la poésie française au XVIème siècle,* Gustave Michaut strives to find the sources for all of Mlle de Scudéry's assertions because he seems to deny the fact that she had any ability to make literary judgements. His study, on the contrary, discloses that for the most part Mlle de Scudéry has utilized her own reading and her own personal comments. This *Tableau* evidently allows us, once again, to appreciate Mlle de Scudéry's immense culture, and it clarifies for us her literary tastes, since she often takes the trouble to explain the reasoning behind her opinion.

In comparing these pages with those of *Clélie* (VIII, 850 et seq.) where the "Histoire d'Hésiode" also included a "Tableau de la poésie française," one can see that Mlle de Scudéry's opinions had not changed; they merely became more assured. Whereas in *Clélie* she limited herself to speaking about poetry, in "L'Histoire du Comte d'Albe" she also includes mention of authors of prose, and she expresses her extreme admiration for Amyot and Montaigne. This probably was not a surprise to her readers, who most likely had already noticed that she borrowed freely from Amyot's translation of Plutarch, and that she made allusions to Montaigne, which regularly appeared in the various volumes of her *Conversations morales.* This clearly indicates that she read these authors diligently.

As far as poetry is concerned, she recalls, once again, the grandeur of the *poésie provençale,* and mentions that even the princes had pleasure in composing poetry in that language. Turning to French poetry she expresses her admiration for Ronsard and du Bellay, if with some reservation. In the discussion that follows the reading of a short account of Ronsard's life, it is mentioned that his verses were too scholarly and contained too much material borrowed from the Ancients. One can suppose that Mlle de Scudéry's own opinion can be seen in this defense of his genius:

I have heard Ronsard say that he is the enemy of vulgar thoughts, that prose is the language of men and poetry that of the gods. To strengthen this position he asserts that Michelangelo, an excellent sculptor, said that a perfect painting should approximate as closely as possible a beautiful sculpture, but that, on the contrary, sculpture should remove itself as far as possible from paintings. By the same token, while prose can sometimes adorn itself with elements of poetry, poems must always lift themselves above the level of prose and avoid as much as possible its simplicity." ("Comte d'Albe," 59)

In his commentary on the *Tableau de la poésie française*, Gustave Michaut implied that Mlle de Scudéry wrote this defense of Ronsard in order to refute Boileau's *L'Art poétique*, which attacked the great poet. Although it is within the realm of possibility to see this as an answer to Boileau, it does seem strange that Mlle de Scudéry would wait ten years to make it. It is equally important to remember that Mlle de Scudéry and her friends admired Ronsard long before the publication of *L'Art poétique*. In *Clélie* (VIII, 852) she speaks of his genius and of the beauty of the *Hymnes*, noting, however, his role of forerunner, which hindered him from attaining the perfection that would have been his had he lived in a later period. This opinion was shared by Pellisson, who also had a marked preference for *Les Hymnes*, particularly *Les Hymnes des quatre saisons*, if one is to believe his correspondence.[15] In the *Discours* that accompanies the *Oeuvres de Jean-François Sarasin*, Pellisson speaks of the grandeur of sixteenth century poetry.[16] His biographer has commented that he was, at times, quite critical of his contemporaries because of his admiration for the authors of antiquity and of the Renaissance.[17]

Chapelain, too, recognized Ronsard's greatness, but he also mentioned the limitations that his era imposed on him: "He had genius but it only appeared when he did not try to show off his knowledge, and it is a pity . . . that this natural ability and fertile imagination did not develop in a time like ours. Even though one must follow certain rules, he still has artistic freedom."[18]

Ronsard's genius, therefore, was acknowledged by certain *Précieux*, although his scholarly vocabulary and his references to mythology disturbed the majority of them. It certainly is not necessary to assume that Mlle de Scudéry's interest in Ronsard was motivated by a desire to use him as a weapon against Boileau. She is simply expressing, once again, her tastes, and she was not the only one to have such opinions.

The group that she describes in "L'Histoire du Comte d'Albe," however, feels much more in harmony with poets of a less majestic style. Marot is found to be "ingeniously pleasant" (*Tableau*, 46) and one of the women in the group declares: "Despite the admiration I have for Ronsard, I can do without Greeks when reading about love, and Desportes has a natural sweetness that is more pleasing in this type of poetry" (*Tableau*, 70). The group praises Bertaut even more. They sing several of his songs and at the end of a couplet the hostess exclaims: "It is quite beautiful, and what makes it beautiful is that it is so natural, both in content and in expression" (*Tableau*, 86).

If Maurice Scève and Louise Labé are not included in the *Tableau*, *Les Dames* des Roches are cited as models of the "*bel esprit féminin*." Doubtlessly there is a similarity between their *salon* and that of Mlle de Scudéry, which she easily recognized, and she has the good humor to include the story of "the flea" that inspired so many poems written by several important men (*Tableau*, 52–54).

Mlle de Scudéry also demonstrated a great knowledge of civilization and of historical events. She briefly mentions *L'Académie du Palais*, which met three times a week at the court of Henri III, and included some women "who were more intelligent than the usual members of their sex" (*Tableau*, 76). It seems that this is perhaps a comment on the fact that despite her glory and the vastness of her culture, of which she has given so much evidence in this part of the story of the Comte d'Albe, she nevertheless was never invited to attend the meetings of *L'Académie* of the seventeenth century.

The various *nouvelles* written by Mlle de Scudéry after her epic novels show a continuation of the themes that she treated throughout her career, particularly those dealing with love, women, and marriage. The evolution of society, however, led to a transformation of the psychology regarding heroines and heroes. If the heroines in the epic novels tried to avoid marriage, it was because the high value they placed on themselves prevented them from rewarding their faithful suitors. Despite their prowess as warriors, the men never really deserved the women. In the *nouvelles* the suitors, although valiant, do not have to accomplish the deeds that Ibrahim, Cyrus, or Aronce placed at the feet of their beloveds. The hero marries the heroine if he is able to convince her of his eternal love.

In this second half of the seventeenth century the heroine has lost the preeminence she had during the *Fronde*. She has become more humble and more afraid to give herself to a man who might scorn her after marriage. Mlle de Scudéry's heroines, just like Madame de Clèves, who is the incarnation of this fear and of the renunciation it inspires, also feel the temptation to say no. Mlle de Scudéry, however, was much more optimistic than Mme de Lafayette, and these later heroines, like Isabelle, Mandane, and Clélie before them, choose to run the risks of marriage and trust in what life has in store for them.

CHAPTER 4

# Other Facets of Mlle de Scudéry's Literary Talents

E VEN though she is known mainly as a novelist, Mlle de Scudéry
   also had other literary talents. For some she was most out-
standing as a moralist, and for others, such as Voltaire, it was as a
poet that she excelled.

## I Les Discours

A. *Les Harangues héroïques ou Les Femmes illustres*
    It is not known with certainty exactly what part Mlle de Scudéry
played in the writing of this work, published by Georges de Scudéry
in 1642. Tallemant has stated that she wrote a part of it, but Bosquillon has not included it among her works. It utilizes the same
format as Manzini's *Les Harangues ou Discours académiques*, which
Georges de Scudéry had just translated. It is comprised of two
volumes. The first one consists of discourses supposedly composed
by famous women. The second is a defense of certain ideas, such as
"honor is preferable to love" or "appearances are deceiving" or "he
who has not suffered cannot know pleasure."
    Given the fact that Mlle de Scudéry was also known as Sapho, and
that one of the discourses in the first part of the work is attributed to
the Greek poetess (423–41), it is tempting to believe that she did
have a role in its composition. This notion is further strengthened by
the fact that many of the ideas expressed in the discourse are found
in her later works.
    The style is well defined and quite feminist in tone. Without
having the causticity of certain works found in the sixteenth century
118

*Querelle des Femmes*, which seek to prove the superiority of women, this discourse takes a more reasonable position. It speaks of equality, much like Mlle de Gournay did twenty years before in her *Egalité des hommes et des femmes*. The tone that Sapho strikes in her discourse is rather subdued, and the arguments are based mainly on fact.

Sapho is directing her speech to the young Erinne, and seeks to encourage her to overcome the lack of confidence that many women have in regard to their talents. She further wishes to rid her of the false notion that even if she did have certain gifts, being a woman she should not use them. It is pointed out that, except for physical strength, men and women are born equally gifted. Men are doubtlessly stronger than women, but it is also true that among animals the weakest is often the most ingenious. This could easily be applied to human beings as well. Furthermore, it makes little sense to say that nature gives beauty to women and intelligence to men. All one has to do is to look around and see all of the ugly women and the stupid men to realize how illogical this supposition is. Since women have enough intelligence to be able to apply themselves to literature, why should they refrain from doing so? The shame does not lie in writing verse, but in doing it badly, and this shame can be applied to any bad poet, whether it be a man or a woman.

If Erinne is capable of writing beautiful lines, she will assure herself of immortality because art confers on its creators "a beauty that neither time, old age, or death itself can ever take away" (I, 436). Instead of waiting for poets to immortalize her beauty, a woman should create works that will of themselves establish her immortality.

B. *Discours de la gloire*

With this text Mlle de Scudéry won first prize in a contest organized by the *Académie française.* It was established in memory of Balzac, who had determined the format to be followed in the discourse. The title under which it was published is misleading. In fact, the subject imposed on the writer was: "On praise and on glory; that they belong exclusively to God and that men are usually their usurpers. *Non nobis, Domine, non nobis, sed nomine tuo da gloriam.*"

The text was sent anonymously to Conrart and was signed only with a special mark that would later identify the author. It is certain that the content of the text ran little risk of divulging Mlle de Scudéry's identity because she followed Balzac's ideas precisely. For him glory did not exist without praise, and since man is, by nature, imperfect, his "mind limited," and his "judgement faulty," glory could never really appertain to him but only to God.

As Professor Sutcliffe has pointed out,[1] Mlle de Scudéry, whether in her *Conversations* or in her novels, utilizes an entirely different notion of glory. First of all, it is not necessarily linked to one's reputation, as is indicated in this passage from *Clélie*, and repeated in the *Conversations morales:*

Glory is something that is the result of a virtuous action as much as light is a result of the sun that produces it, and, like the light from the sun, does not depend on any external stimuli. Since a virtuous action does not need to be witnessed in order to be what it is, it necessarily follows that glory, which is born of this action, will infallibly follow even though the action has not been publicized. It is better to find glory in one's own merit. In fact it is more important to have self-respect than to gain respect from others, and it is better to earn glory than to publicize it. (*Clélie* III, 480–81)

When she expresses her own ideas, then, Mlle de Scudéry obviously differs from the position held by Balzac. She is much closer to Montaigne's definition of glory, expressed in *Les Essais* (II, xvi)[2], and to Descartes in his treatise *Des passions de l'âme.* The only reason that man can have to feel self-esteem, according to Descartes, is the use of his free will and the control he has over his desires.[3] This is clearly the direction that Mlle de Scudéry takes when she comments on the situation that Clélie finds herself in when she is threatened by marriage to a man she detests: "If a feeling of glory had not placed in her heart the necessary strength to rise above herself, she doubtlessly would have acted in a different manner" (*Clélie* I, 506). Because of her self-respect, Clélie found the strength to resist certain impulses, and this action evidently would never be known by anyone. This tends to negate the "praise" aspect of glory and emphasizes the value of a choice made of one's own free will, in the privacy of one's own conscience.

Her personal ideas, then, are in opposition to the theory she maintained in the *Discours,* and this work should be regarded for what it is: an exercise in style. Mlle de Scudéry's own opinions truly come to light in her volumes of conversations.

## II   Les Conversations morales[4]

In his *La Politesse mondaine et les théories de l'honnêteté*[5] Maurice Magendie indicated the large number of works concerning the subject of morals that were published in the seventeenth century. Among the Ancients, special attention was given to Plutarch. The Amyot translation of *Les Oeuvres morales et mêlées* was reprinted twelve times between the years 1600 and 1660. Foreign writers such as Erasmus, Vivès, Castiglione, and Guevara were also read, and French works dealing with the subject were not lacking. Du Souhait, Nervèze, Pasquier, du Refuge, Faret, and Grenailles all contributed. Their treatises, however, dealt mainly with lessons on how to succeed at court or in society.

This last category, so didactic in spirit, was quite different from the style of Mlle de Scudéry's *Conversations*. They were much more in keeping, as regards inspiration, with the works of Plutarch, Erasmus, or Montaigne. Nowadays we tend to forget the great number of works in the seventeenth century that were dedicated to the study of morals and behavior, of which La Rochefoucauld's *Maximes et Réflexions*, La Bruyère's *Caractères*, and Pascal's *Les Pensées*, though different in their goals, are the best remembered. Mlle de Scudéry, who attended Mme de Sablé's salon along with La Rochefaucauld and Pascal, shared their interest in this subject, but the format she used was quite different.

The way in which the *Conversations* are presented offers a reproduction of the *société précieuse*, with a meeting of friends generally providing the framework in which certain questions are discussed in a rather informal manner. Some conversations are original, but a number of them have been taken verbatim from her fictional works. Brief stories are told in order to make certain points, but a solution is rarely given. The reader, just like the personage in the salon, is presented with various arguments and then must make up his own mind. This genre is, in many ways, reminiscent of the discussions that precede and follow the stories in Marguerite de Navarre's *Heptaméron*.

The style of these conversations is generally quite vivacious, and Mlle de Scudéry seems to have put in them many of her own opinions. They are, therefore, of great interest today because they allow us a clearer understanding of the customs and ideas of seventeenth century France.

A. *Philosophy*

At several points Mlle de Scudéry clearly expresses her rejection of philosophical systems. Although judging from the evidence, she read the theoretical works of many philosophers and had herself ventured into the world of the abstract in her *Discours de la gloire,* she refused to make a habit of it. In fact, there are numerous references throughout her works that make light of philosophers and their insistence that they alone had found the truth. In the "Histoire de Bélinde," she describes the young woman's unhappiness over the loss of a friend "who immersed herself so deeply in ancient and modern philosophy that Epicurus' atoms and Descartes' vortices had caused her to vanish. Bélinde did not wish to follow her into a labyrinth from which one almost never leaves without losing the way" (M, 417).[6]

In *Les Entretiens de morale,* she goes even further and explains that she refuses to involve herself in the dispute regarding Descartes' vortices. This dispute actually deals with an argument "that is revived from century to century and which will last forever because it is so vast and so beyond the reach of the human mind that there will always be some unforeseen difficulties mixed with half truths. The reason for this is that philosophers generally try to say what has never been said, rather than to try to say the truth" (E, 211).

Descartes is not the only philosopher of whom she is distrustful. She also scoffs at Democritus and his theory of atoms, as well as at Pythagoras' views on the transmigration of souls (CN, 173). The mention of Pythagoras leads to a conversation in regard to vegetarians: "You would have highly approved" says one of the discussants, "of this philosopher . . . whose disciples ate neither meat nor fish." "It is true," replies Clarice, "that if it were not so generally accepted and so habitual, nothing would be more horrible than to kill an animal in order to survive. If I had not already been accustomed to such an idea, I would never have thought it necessary to kill so many animals that do not in any way cause us harm" (E, 171). Clarice further adds that it is perfectly feasible to nourish oneself with vegetables and fruit.

Her adversaries utilize the two arguments that are still heard today for justifying the slaughter of animals: "One reason is the divine authority that expressly gives animals to man to do with as he pleases, and the other is that if society does not kill animals they will eventually kill man or deplete his sources of food" (E, 171).

This interest in vegetarianism is but one expression of Mlle de Scudéry's great love for all types of creatures. Martin Lister wrote about two chameleons that had been sent to her from Egypt: "In winter she lodged them in cotton, and in the fiercest weather she put them under a bowl of copper full of hot water."[7] She managed to keep them alive for four years. This concern for animals explains why Mlle de Scudéry was so strongly against Descartes' theory of the Beast-Machine. Both she and Descartes' own niece shared a correspondence, sometimes in verse, that decried that inhumane theory.[8]

Having spent a part of her youth in the country, Mlle de Scudéry had probably always loved animals. She most likely did not acquire this love in the same way as Mme de Rambouillet, who was heard to say that she "learned to love animals because they were never capable of being ungrateful as man was" (M, 418). Mlle de Scudéry was greatly in harmony with nature and this can also be seen in the love she had for flowers. Living on the outskirts of the Marais, she was able to have a beautiful garden. She cultivated many plants, such as jasmine, oleanders, and dwarf orange trees, which were difficult to grow in the Parisian climate. She also loved flowers of the forest and particularly the lily-of-the-valley: "I love even the simplest of wild flowers. Even though it is found only in the woods and does not adorn our gardens, I find the lily-of-the-valley to be the most beautiful of flowers and to have the most pleasant aroma" (E, 154).

Her love of nature however, did not cause her to yearn for a life of solitude. In one of the conversations a personage defends the idea of leaving society in order to find peace. He maintains that only an agricultural existence avoids the development of man's evil passions: "War, whether just or injust, is filled with horror, business with fraud and deceit, and there is less public safety in our largest cities. All courts, large or small, are filled with those who are ambitious or envious, who are scandalmongers or slanderers, who are sensualists or libertines, but an agricultural existence harms no one and does not at all provide a stimulus for human failings" (E, 172).

It does not seem that Mlle de Scudéry shares this rather negative view. Her feelings on the matter are probably expressed in this response: "I admit that the source of all passions is found in the human heart, and these passions are larger or smaller depending upon situations that come from without . . ." (E, 173). This means that man himself has the possibility of choosing between good and evil, and he should not let circumstances lead him in the wrong direction. Another character in the *Conversations nouvelles* asks if it is really possible to control one's passions, and the answer is un-equivocal: "Have no doubt that passions are controlled by reason and by virtue in a well-intentioned heart" (C.N. 224).

This belief in the theory that man has control over his actions is clearly expressed throughout Mlle de Scudéry's novels. There are, however, some monstrous women, such as Roxelane, Thomiris, or Tullie, who are magnificent in their iniquity. Despite the greatness of these characters, their actions are clearly condemned because the moral value of one's deeds can never be forgotten. Here again we see the separation of glory and reputation clearly manifested. Tullie is the queen and is admired, but although she is praised, she has no part of glory. In the *Conversations nouvelles* there is a discussion about a man who has been unjustly exiled. The group comments that he must be quite unhappy, but Mlle de Scudéry is of a different opinion: "One cannot think him unhappy if he is blameless and can live with his own conscience" (CN, 212).

Mlle de Scudéry acknowledges that passion does exist, but she always clearly indicates that it must be curbed when morally dangerous. This seems to be in contradiction with Adam's[9] beliefs on the matter. He feels that she advocated satisfying passions rather than resisting them. Naturally this sort of reasoning can be found in certain of Mlle de Scudéry's characters, as in the case of Bajazet's evil advice to Roxelane, but it is limited to a few cases and the reader is always aware that one is dealing with villains and villainesses.

She recognized, then, the existence of profound forces in man that dispose him toward good or evil, but she was equally aware of man's capability to judge and to choose. One of her characters who does attain a kind of perfection is Anténor, who lives alone with his books. He makes this comment: "All of my inclinations are so con-trolled by my good sense that I enjoy a tranquillity that nothing can upset. I feel no love, no hate, no ambition, and I spend my life admiring the beauty of the universe" (CN, 353).

Mlle de Scudéry loved society too much to have recommended this sort of existence for everyone, but Anténor does represent the model of the man who has totally dominated his passions. He can now enjoy the beauties of creation, and the idea of creation is one that is often found in Mlle de Scudéry's works. On many occasions she speaks of the divine architect, whose presence can be discerned in all things large or small: "Can we not see that the admirable architect who created the world also thought to adorn it? Why else do we have trees and shrubs that give us flowers but bear no fruit?" (E, 184). She was fascinated with butterflies and described the myriad colors of their wings with precision and brilliance (E, 395). The beauty of the peacock provided, to her way of thinking, enough evidence to show "that the world was not created haphazardly and that even the smallest part of the universe, when examined, gives proof positive of this" (E, 175).

Mlle de Scudéry goes on to say that man in his smallness is unable to judge the whole of creation. Oftentimes that which man, with his limited outlook, considers to be bad may have redeeming features: "I believe that everything considered dangerous to man has some good qualities that are not readily seen" (E, 185). She cites as an example the case of the viper which is, to be sure, a noxious creature, but from which a substance can be extracted that serves as an aid against fainting spells.

Admitting, then, that our understanding of the universe is limited, Mlle de Scudéry feels that this prayer by Socrates is the only reasonable request that man can make of God: "O Jupiter, even if we do not ask for it, grant us what is good, and even if we ask for it, do not give us what is bad" (CN, 104).


B. *Society Life*

Mlle de Scudéry loved society life, but her circle had to be a select one: "What I find most agreeable is to be in the company of five or six friends who put aside all worrisome thoughts and look at the good life as something that brings them together and unites them. It gives them a true sense of freedom that leads to joy and allows them to find all the pleasures they are seeking" (CN, 154). To live in society means to observe its customs, but one should not be a slave to them. The basis for urbanity is "the desire to please" (CN, 180) and, according to Mlle de Scudéry, Mme de Rambouillet was the personification of *politesse*. She was "the one woman in the world who best understood urbanity. She inspired it in all those who saw her, and while she lived it spread from her salon to the court and then throughout the kingdom. What remains of it today has come from her" (CN, 122).

From this point the group tries to find a general definition of *politesse:*

True urbanity means to know how to live and how to say the right thing at the right moment. It means to comply with certain customs at the possible expense of common sense. . . . To be urbane is never to be rude or uncivil to anyone, and never to say to others what you would not wish them to say to you. One should also not want to monopolize a conversation by speaking constantly. An audacious air should always be avoided, as well as a scornful silence, and one should never indulge in ridiculous familiarities of which we have so many examples today. . . . One must know ethics in order to understand urbanity. (CN, 126–29)

Urbanity requires a respect for customs and propriety, but intelligence and good judgement equally play a part. Mlle de Scudéry considers certain practices to be tyrannical and ridiculous. She cites an amusing example of a country where "the husbands are bedridden while the wives are having their babies!" (M, 102). She has also noted the extreme variation in customs among different countries depending upon historical period and type of climate: "It is true that customs change according to climate and country. Most of the time we share the beliefs that our fathers held without really fathoming the reason behind them" (CN, 167).

For her own account, Mlle de Scudéry observed the rules of *politesse* and believed that customs formed a kind of framework that allowed people in society to have more pleasant relationships in a milieu where everyone knew the rules of the game. She did, however, find some of these customs amusing, and even mocked them at times. One of her favorite targets was the ridiculous manner in which some people spoke.

The word "impertinent" for example, which Molière made fun of in *Les Précieuses ridicules,* also aroused a protest from Mlle de Scudéry in regard to the word's improper usage: "This expression began in the law courts before moving to the city and finally to the palace, where it is presently more in use than in the law courts themselves. . . . Impertinent things in a lawyer's plea really meant things that were of no use to the trial or which do not pertain to the case at hand. . . . Little by little the usage of this word has come to mean that if an action is unreasonable or improper it can be called impertinent" (E, 258–59). Mlle de Scudéry could not help but smile when someone said "the wind is impertinent," but, on the other hand, she assures us that the painter who depicted Judith holding Holofernes' head aloft with a view of crosses on church steeples in the background was truly guilty of impertinence! (E, 266)

This, of course, was not the only word or expression that amused Mlle de Scudéry. She also noted the appearance of these new expressions: *Le grand air, le bel air, le bon air, le savoir-faire,* and the famous *faire attention* (M, 105). Far from being responsible for these innovations, Mlle de Scudéry was not even convinced of their value.

Even though a poet herself, she derided certain abuses in poetic literature. An example she gives is the type of poem in which the poet first says: "If you leave, Iris, I will die of sorrow," only to add afterward: "But if I see you again I will die of joy." Another topic of conversation was the reemergence of old poetic forms such as the *rondeau,* brought back to popularity by Voiture (M, 104); and still another subject was the psychology involved in the reasons that led Auguste to pardon Cinna in the play by Corneille.

There is also a discussion of painting and the importance of the limitation that nature places on this art form. Mlle de Scudéry's opinion on this matter seems to have been expressed in this comment: "In portraits I look for an honest resemblance . . . and beautifully vivid colors in all other paintings" (M, 36). In architecture she admired Mansart's constructions and was astonished by the wonder of the *Galerie des Glaces* at the Château of Versailles (C.N, 20).

This kind of subject matter was just touched upon in passing in order to illustrate one's opinion. On the contrary, problems of a psychological nature provided the basis for numerous conversations in which there was an attempt to define and to judge the feelings that occupy the human soul. For example, anger is a fault, but "it is not a treacherous emotion that lies hidden at the bottom of one's heart like envy" (M, 135). The cause of impatience is analyzed: "It is a weakness of the heart and mind and a kind of well-hidden *amour-propre* that causes us to want everything to accomodate itself to us without our accomodating ourselves to anything. Instead of patiently accepting what we cannot prevent we rebel against it, and our senses mutter in protest instead of submitting" (E, 92). In discussing *libéralité* it is concluded that "if one is not generous when young, he will not fail to be a miser when old" (M, 294).

Often there are discussions on a comparison of certain qualities.

What is the difference between joy and vivacity, generosity and magnanimity, goodness and gentleness? Many conversations deal with friendship, and there is this rather lofty definition of what Mlle de Scudéry feels to be the most noble of sentiments: "The mark of perfect friendship is the sharing, without exception, of all one's possessions" (M, 428). Not all friendships are so perfect, but they are necessary if one is to have a happy life. It is noteworthy that the subject of friendship was one that greatly occupied many of the *Précieux*, and Mme de Sablé's group dedicated numerous encounters to the study of this sentiment and its manifestations. They discussed what the limits of friendship should be, and Arnauld d'Andilly even defended the idea that one should be more loyal to a friend than to one's country.[10]

## C. *Women*

A subject that is of particular interest to us today is the condition of women in society. As has already been mentioned, Mlle de Scudéry had strongly feminist views, some of which would certainly not be out of date today. Why, she asks, can men be ugly but not women? "It would seem that women are placed on earth for the same purpose as colors—merely to please the eye" (CN, 144). A man taking part in the conversation replies that it is possible to love a plain woman providing that she is not too ugly. "One's eyes eventually get used to anything, and one can find a woman whose mind is so beautiful and whose disposition is so charming that she will be extremely pleasing and much loved" (CN, 148).

Mlle de Scudéry was scornful of certain so-called feminine qualities, such as beauty and sweetness, if they were not accompanied by other, more solid, attributes. "I assure you that when I hear that a woman is only beautiful and quite sweet I am not really certain just what that means, and I visualize a beautiful simpleton listening to 'sweet nothings' said to her by the first man to arrive" (CN, 246). Mlle de Scudéry always encouraged women to develop their intelligence, to learn to read, and to be able to take part in discussions with friends of their choice. A woman can then attain a certain intellectual independence. She will not be just a wife or a mother but will be, according to the feminist viewpoint, a real individual.

Another concept that has a great deal of relevance today is Mlle de Scudéry's advice on how to prepare for old age. For women whose charm lies entirely in physical beauty, old age can be a difficult time of life. They no longer receive the attention of gallant suitors, and so must dedicate themselves to running a household or to an often false piety.

In the *Entretiens de morale* there is a portrait of the opposite kind of older woman. Chrysante is a type of "liberated old lady," and she clearly states her philosophy on aging: "Beginning with my youth I have profited from the experience of others. . . . Ever since the springtime of my life I have thought of providing myself with all that might render the winter less disagreeable" (E, 134). She finds it strange that women will take care to protect themselves from the cold but will not think of what they can do to make old age less troublesome for themselves and for those close to them.

Mlle de Scudéry was quite aware, then, of the circumstances the women of her epoch found themselves in, and gave them valuable advice in the way to add meaning to their lives. This advice has a strangely modern tone, and extracts of her comments in regard to old age would not at all be out of place today in a publication destined for those of the *troisième âge*.

Naturally, her advice also encompassed the problems of marriage. Throughout her works she commented that marriage is an important undertaking and difficult to succeed in. The persons considering this step should make this decision themselves, and not leave it to their parents to decide for them. Since it is a decision that will most likely affect the rest of their lives, it should be made only after a great deal of circumspection. The regret that divorce was not allowed in her time can be clearly seen in *Les Entretiens de morale*, where Mlle de Scudéry wrote: "The ancient Romans, who permitted divorce, were not wrong" (E, 142). She protected herself against criticism from the church, however, by adding that while in ancient times a marriage was a simple contract, it had since become a sacrament. Nevertheless, her feminine readers, considering marriage, most likely were apt to think twice before making the final decision.

## D. *Louis XIV, The Hero Personified*

In studying the evolution of ideas in the seventeenth century it is interesting to note that Mlle de Scudéry's novels were all dedicated to important women of her time, but her *Conversations*, after 1684, were dedicated to the king. The century saw the passage from an heroic epoch in which any person could be a hero if endowed with the proper virtue and inspiration, to the time in which heroism was concentrated solely in the person of the king. Mlle de Scudéry was perfectly aware of this transition. Instead of depicting several heroes, each one more valiant than the other, she began to sing the glory of one hero, and that, of course, was Louis XIV.[11]

In a discussion found in *Les Conversations nouvelles* regarding *politesse*, she explains that *politesse*, or urbanity, develops better in a monarchy than in a republic. Urbanity comes from the desire to please, and since in a monarchy everyone is trying to please one person, a certain uniformity of manners is the result (CN, 180).

The king also brings about a uniformity of tastes and opinions. "It is good that in a monarchy the sovereign is like the pilot of a vessel in which all the crew sleeps in security without the need to study the stars or man the wheel" (CN, 184). The king instructs his subjects, and shows them by his own example that diversions should not be the sole occupation of life. "Although he spends some hours in the pleasures of an *honnête homme*, he still does not fail to fulfill the obligations of a great king" (CN, 33).

At the same time, the king has heroic attributes. Only in him can magnificence be found, and it is expressed in a thousand ways, the construction of Versailles being but one (CN, 47). In the *Conversations sur divers sujets* Mlle de Scudéry depicts Louis XIV in all of his glory under the name of Sésostris le Grand (C, 593). In *Clélie* he was depicted as Alcandre, and mention of his greatness was shared with praise for other heroic personages. In the *Conversations* all of the glory is centered in the king alone. Although he is quite gifted in the art of lively banter, he never indulges in it because no one could dare answer him. This symbolizes his position as sovereign of his people. He has become, as in the case of Vigny's *Moïse*, *"puissant et solitaire."*

### III   *Poetry*

Attending the various salons with regularity, Mlle de Scudéry was led to participate in the game of writing impromptu poetry, which was much in vogue among the *Précieux*. These poems were written according to the occasion, and were often discarded afterward. Many of Mlle de Scudéry's poems were not printed in her lifetime and are known today mainly because they were quoted in letters or memoirs that have been passed down to us. Some of her poetry, however, has been included in certain collections, but we certainly do not have the complete poetic output of this prolific poetess, who was still writing impromptu poems at the age of ninety-two.

The circumstances that inspired this poetry could be quite diverse. An example is the epitaph written on the occasion of the death of Badine, the Duke of Roquelaure's dog:

> Ci-gît la célèbre Badine
> Qui n'eut ni bonté ni beauté,
> Mais dont l'esprit a démonté
> Le système de la machine.[12]

("Here lies the famous Badine, who was neither good nor beautiful, but whose intelligence has demolished the theory of the machine.")

This is of course a reference to Descartes' theory that animals were nothing but machines.

On the way to Mme Aragonais' country home, Mlle de Scudéry improvised this much-celebrated poem, which makes fun of the serious Conrart, commenting that despite his solemn exterior he still had a tender spot in his heart for a certain lady. The "landerirette" and "landeriri" are refrains that were used in songs of the time:

> Conrart, sage comme un Caton,
> A pourtant au coeur, ce dit-on,
> Landerirette,
> Un petit endroit attendri,
> Landeriri.[13]

The subject could also be more profound. Nanteuil had painted Mlle de Scudéry's portrait, which has been lost, and he composed a flattering madrigal in which he stated that to have painted her assured him of immortality. Mlle de Scudéry, fully aware that physical beauty was not her strong point, responded with two poems, one of which seemed particularly sincere:

> Nanteuil, en faisant mon image,
> A de son art divin signalé le pouvoir.
> Je hais mes yeux dans mon miroir,
> Je les aime dans son ouvrage. (R, 502)

She praises Nanteuil's ability as a painter, and adds that although she hates her eyes reflected in a mirror, she loves the sight of them in his painting.

One of her two best-known impromptus was dedicated to Condé, the other to Louis XIV. The poem for Condé was written during the *Fronde* when Mlle de Scudéry visited his prison cell. It is entitled: "Impromptu fait au donjon de Vincennes en visitant la chambre où le prince de Condé avait été prisonnier."

> En voyant ces oeillets qu'un illustre guerrier
> Arrosa d'une main qui gagna des batailles,
> Souviens-toi qu'Apollon bâtissait des murailles,
> Et ne t'étonne pas si Mars est jardinier. (R, 509)

Mlle de Scudéry was very impressed with the window box in which some carnations were growing. The poem expresses the thought that since Apollo, who was the god of poetry and music, was also capable of building walls, it is not amazing that such a warrior as Condé could nurture the growth of beautiful flowers by his own hand.

Among the numerous poems written in praise of Louis XIV, this sextain was extremely successful, perhaps because the phrase "a hero for all seasons" was particularly pleasing.

> Les héros de l'antiquité,
> N'étaient que des héros d'été.
> Ils suivaient le printemps comme les hirondelles.
> La victoire en hiver pour eux n'avait pas d'ailes;
> Mais malgré les frimas, la neige et les glaçons,
> Louis est un héros de toutes les saisons. (R, 520)

The poem refers to the fact that ancient heroes only fought their battles in summertime. They followed the spring like swallows, but could not spread their wings in winter. Louis XIV, on the contrary, was not impeded by frost, snow, or ice, and was, therefore, a hero for all seasons.

Certain sad moments in Mlle de Scudéry's life inspired some rather touching poetry, such as these lines written in 1694 upon the death of her old friend, Abbé Boisot.

> Quoi! Cet illustre abbé si bon, si vertueux,
> Si savant, si poli, d'un coeur si généreux,

> Qui connaissait si bien le merveilleux Acante,
> Dont il était aimé d'une amitié constante,
> A subi de la mort les implacables lois!
> Ah! D'un si rare ami la perte surprenante
> Rend ma douleur si violente
> Que je crois perdre Acante une seconde fois. (R, 526)

In this poem she wrote of his knowledge and generosity, and of the closeness of their friendship. The suddenness of his death produced a pain so violent that she felt as though she had lost "Acante a second time," referring, of course, to her beloved Pellisson.

Mlle de Scudéry also included some poems in *Clélie* and in the volumes of *Conversations*. In the eighth volume of *Clélie*, Clymène, who has been abandoned by the ambitious Lysicrate, expresses her sorrow in a touching elegy as the shepherdess Amarillis speaking to her unfaithful Tircis. After having reproached him for his infidelity she concludes:

> Hélas, en ce disant je sens que je soupire
> Et qu'un trouble secret me dit quand je vous vois,
> Que malgré mon dépit mon coeur n'est plus à moi.
> Il murmure et se plaint, mais il veut qu'on l'apaise,
> Par de tendres discours, dont la douceur lui plaise.
> Il cherche à se tromper, trompez-le donc Tircis . . .

Amarillis implores Tircis to return to her. She would rather have him pretend to love her than not to have him at all. "I prefer a hundred fold this pleasant torment than to be without pain and without a lover":

> Aussi bien je mourrais si ma flamme était morte
> Et j'aime mieux cent fois cet aimable tourment
> Que d'être sans douleur et d'être sans amant. (*Clélie*, VIII, 930–32)

In the *Conversations* her poems are more didactic in style. The idea for the four poems dedicated to the seasons came from Ronsard's *Hymnes des quatre saisons*, but their treatment is entirely different. The change in seasons is used by Mlle de Scudéry as a model for what is awaiting mankind, and it serves as a symbol of the need to correct human nature. We protest against the change of seasons, but "without trying to understand ourselves, we never change and want to change everything else." (Et sans nous bien connaître et sans nous corriger/Nous ne changeons jamais et voulons tout changer) (*Tableau*, 104). The poem on summer draws an analogy between the season and the summertime of our lives, when our senses triumph over our reason:

> Tout cède, tout fléchit sous le pouvoir des sens,
> Et l'esprit fait contre eux des efforts impuissants.
> Heureux et très heureux qui peut passer sa vie
> Sans suivre les transports où cet âge convie. (*Tableau*, 108)

Mlle de Scudéry, however, does not condemn pleasures. She criticizes certain excesses and sums up her thoughts with this particularly well-wrought line: "Il faut voir promptement ce qu'on doit voir un jour" ("It would be better to understand promptly that which one must understand eventually").

Autumn is represented as the ideal time of man's life:

> Le bon sens règle enfin jusques à nos désirs
> Et résiste sans peine aux charmes des plaisirs.
> Mais pour les passions si sujettes à nuire
> Songez à les régler au lieu de les détruire.
> L'art de s'en bien servir est un art précieux. (*Tableau*, 110)

In this time of a person's life he should enjoy a useful serenity. Now good sense regulates his desires and allows him to resist excessive pleasures. He should not destroy passion, however, but rather utilize the good in it. To be able to do this is a precious art indeed.

Mlle de Scudéry rarely chose to attempt serious poetry. One of these occasions, however, came at the time of Fouquet's disgrace. Her elegy on "the subject of M. Fouquet" resounded with brilliance in the general silence that surrounded the event. In this poem she affirms once again her respect for Fouquet and lauds the fact that he was as great in adversity as he was when in power. She describes his fall from grace with beauty and eloquence:

> Le ciel était serein quand ce grand coup de foudre
> A mis tous ces desseins et sa fortune en poudre
> Mais parmi les horreurs qui l'ont environné
> Ce coup, qui l'a surpris, ne l'a pas étonné:
> Il savait que le sort des humaines misères
> Joint aux plus grands plaisirs des peines plus amères.

> Que rien sous le soleil n'est durable et constant,
> Que la cour n'est enfin qu'un empire flottant,
> Où dans un même jour les grands vaisseaux échouent
> Dessus les mêmes flots où les barques se jouent.[14]

Fouquet found that his soul was freer in prison than it had been at court. He had always known the inherent danger of his position with the king and likens the court to an ocean, upon which the large vessels can go aground and be destroyed while smaller boats will survive. He had the inner strength to remain serene despite his difficulties and even to regard his enemies' triumph with indifference. "Il les voit sans envie et sans inimitié/ Et ses persécuteurs mêmes lui font pitié." Fouquet is able to view his accusers without envy or animosity and can even feel pity for them.

Needless to say, these lines were not without a certain panache, and it certainly took some courage on Mlle de Scudéry's part to have flung them in Colbert's face. She was, however, diplomatic enough to disassociate the king from Fouquet's persecutors. In fact, Fouquet's only regret was that the king was able to interpret his actions as criminal. While he does not know what his crime was, "he thinks himself criminal, if he has displeased the king."

The elegy closes with an adroit appeal to Louis XIV for clemency for what Mlle de Scudéry calls "this innocent crime." Refusing to acknowledge any guilt on Fouquet's part, she asks the king to try to see more clearly and to "pierce the clouds with one sharp glance and dissipate the black vapors that hide the truth in their perfidious shadows":

> Perçant d'un seul regard les nuages épais,
> Et les noires vapeurs de qui les voiles sombres
> Cachent la vérité sous leurs perfides ombres.

Mlle de Scudéry's poetry was inspired by particular circumstances in her life. This gives us the opportunity to study her spontaneous reactions to certain events, such as the visit to Condé's prison cell or the death of Abbé Boisot. The *Conversations*, however, express her ideas in a much different manner. In them she reutilized, in effect, what she considered to be the most interesting discussions from her novels, and added new material that probably gives us an insight into the opinions she formed in her later years.

The basis for her ideas does not seem to have varied much, even though it does reflect certain changes in the beliefs of her contemporaries. Although her treatment of heroes and heroines was greatly modified, she did not, however, give in to the rising pessimism of the time. Until the end of her long life she continued to be inspired by her enthusiasm and her *joie de vivre*, a notion that seems to have gone out of style at the end of the seventeenth century.

## CHAPTER 5

# The Destiny of Mlle de Scudéry's Works

## I Seventeenth Century France

### A. Until circa 1660

RAYMOND Picard has correctly said: "There was a vast public of novel addicts in the seventeenth century, but many of these were ashamed of their craving."[1] Mme de Sévigné's attitude on this subject is among the most classic; she confesses her love for novels, "those silly things," as though she were admitting to a weakness.[2] This attitude was not uncommon, and until the second third of the century the reading public was enthusiastically fond of the type of novel popularized by d'Urfé with his L'Astrée. This novel, written at the beginning of the century, set the standard for those to follow even if it did typify a genre that was considered second rate. It followed the format of Amadis, which included a main plot that was extended through ten or twelve volumes, and throughout which there were developments that had to be resolved at a later time. Furetière has written in Le Roman bourgeois that the authors, in describing their progress, would say "I am at the eighth abduction," instead of saying, "I have got to volume eight."[3]

Mlle de Scudéry, writing in the style of the time, naturally used this technique. Another convention of the period was the use of subplots. Although in Cyrus the main plot is concerned with Cyrus' love for Mandane, and in Clélie with the romance between Clélie and Aronce, other stories were also inserted that were really small novels in their own right. In many cases, however, it was necessary to wait for the dénouement of the principal story in order to learn the outcome of the lesser ones.

In writing novels such as these, Mlle de Scudéry was merely responding to the taste of her readers. She mentioned in Cyrus (X, 367) the fact that her readers did not want a novel to "end short" after only five volumes; they would only be satisfied with a dozen. It is certain that she, indeed, satisfied her public as is demonstrated by the numerous editions that were published by Courbé, and which made him a rich man. The list of reprinted works prepared by Georges Mongrédien for *Revue d'Histoire Littéraire de la France* is long and impressive. The following excerpt from the *Histoire des Dames illustres* further indicates that her books were not only read in the salons, but were also a very popular item in the renting libraries: "Don't we see that Mlle de Scudéry's books are held in the highest esteem and that they are rented at a higher price than the works of renowned historians? The booksellers are asking a rental of a *demi-pistole* for only one volume of this illustrious scholar's works."[4]

This success was also evident in the highest ranks of society. In a letter of December 30, 1650, Sarasin related that Mme de Longueville, having taken refuge at Stenay during the *Fronde*, still managed to read daily the newly–arrived latest volume of *Cyrus* (R, 430). Mme de Lafayette had the same enthusiasm for Sapho's novels. In a letter written to Ménage she asked him to procure for her the fifth volume of *Clélie*, which had just been released. She also included a message for Mlle de Scudéry: "Assure her that I hold her in the highest possible esteem and that I feel for her a great deal of affection—something that I ordinarily feel not at all."[5] Mme de Sévigné shared the same feelings and praised Mlle de Scudéry with these words: "Her wit and acuteness of mind are without limit."[6] In 1684 Mme de Sévigné, in a letter to Mlle de Scudéry herself, wrote of "the adoration" she had for her extraordinary merit: "Thinking of your excellence I am happy to have the friendship and esteem of such a person."[7]

The testimonials of admiration for Mlle de Scudéry are many, and they seem to have been addressed as well to the woman as to the novelist and author of poetry. La Fontaine, for example, confessed in a *Ballade* written in 1665 that he took "great delight in love stories." He notably cited *Cyrus* and the *Carte du Tendre* along with *L'Astrée*, *Polexandre*, and Chrétien de Troyes' *Perceval le Gallois*. In *Le Songe de Vaux* he paid homage, however discreetly, to Mlle de Scudéry's description of the castle in *Clélie*.[8] In *Les Caractères*, La Bruyère, in the chapter entitled "Des Jugements," affirmed that it was possible to be both well bred and knowledgeable at the same time. To support this statement he cited Bossuet and

Scudéry as examples, specifying in a footnote that he was referring to Mlle de Scudéry.[9] In glancing through her correspondence one encounters almost everyone of importance in Europe at the time, and this included the political world as well as the intelligentsia.[10]

Some letters give us evidence that Mlle de Scudéry also had relationships with certain authors that one would not ordinarily associate with her. We know, for example, that Mlle de Scudéry knew Pascal. She might have met him when his young sister Jacqueline performed in Georges de Scudéry's *Le Prince déguisé*, or perhaps later at Mme de Sablé's salon, which they both frequented.[11] Antoine Adam has commented that Mlle de Scudéry was such a regular attendant of this elegant salon, also a favorite meeting place of La Rochefoucauld, that she could be considered a disciple of this eminent exponent of *Préciosité*.[12]

In the *Provinciale* of February 2, 1656, Pascal reproduced a letter from a woman in which she expressed her admiration for the first "Lettre écrite à un provincial" and he commented: "You would like to know the identity of this person who has written in such a manner, but content yourself with honoring her without knowing her, and if you knew her you would honor her even more."[13] If one is to believe what Racine wrote in the "Lettre à l'auteur des Hérésies imaginaires,"[14] this note was from Mlle de Scudéry. Racine said that since she had written in *Clélie* a sympathetic description of the *Solitaires* of Port-Royal, Pascal was merely returning the compliment in writing so glowingly of her in *Les Provinciales*. Racine, however, had juggled the dates, conveniently forgetting that in reality Mlle de Scudéry wrote of the *solitaires* after the *Provinciales*. In the dispute that ensued over the publication of Racine's letter, Port-Royal tried to justify, somewhat clumsily, the reading of a novel in so serious a place, but did not deny that Mlle de Scudéry was the author of the note in question.

The high regard that Pascal had for Mlle de Scudéry was not the result of her sympathy for the Jansenists. Even if she did write favorably of Port-Royal, she was certainly not considered a partisan, but was rather following "the tendency of the intelligentsia of the time to be sympathetically disposed toward Jansenism."[15] The gentlemen of Port-Royal, however, were not alone in their admiration of this illustrious novelist and, in fact, Bossuet, Bouhours, Fléchier, Mascaron, all renowned men of the church and whose orthodoxy was never in question, carried on correspondences with

Mlle de Scudéry that clearly demonstrated in what high esteem they held her.[16]

This esteem, of course, was also felt among the majority of the literary figures of the era, and there are many descriptions that clearly testify to this. In *La Prétieuse*, the celebrated work of Abbé de Pure, there is an extremely laudatory picture of Mlle de Scudéry. The abbé, in his usual ambiguous way, seems to have mistakenly attributed *Cyrus* and *Clélie* to Georges de Scudéry, but he wrote glowingly, if in a rather flowering manner, of the sister:

It is well established that one can call Mlle de Scudéry the Muse of our Century. It is necessary at last to give justice to a part of her merit which her modesty has suppressed with perpetual disavowal. . . . However, the obscurity has been dispersed, and at last the admirable person of whom I speak has allowed us to perceive the radiance that has opened our eyes. . . . I would say that she, through only her conversation in which she is so witty and charming, is capable of tarnishing all else, and in stopping the sun itself. . . . I would dare to say that even though her wit is prodigious, her heart still prevails. It is in the heart of this illustrious person that one can find a pure generosity, an unyielding loyalty, and a friendship that is solid and sincere.[17]

In his *Dictionnaire des Prétieuses,* Somaize, too, extols Mlle de Scudéry's modesty. Referring to her as Sophie, he gives this extremely flattering portrait: "Sophie is superior to all others of her sex in regard to wit, facility to write both prose and poetry, and in the knowledge that produces an accomplished intellect. There are few capable men, if any, who don't consider her a worthy rival. . . . Her intelligence and her sweetness attract to her side the greatest and most illustrious of those who write." Among all this praise he treats Mlle de Scudéry's lack of physical beauty in a most cavalier way: He avoids describing her physically by saying that "one already knows well enough how she looks without my having to speak of it."[18]

Another tribute of great value paid to Mlle de Scudéry appeared in Huet's *De l'Origine des romans.* After having discussed both the history of the novel, its objective, and its possible benefits, he expressed his admiration for the great d'Urfé and then passed on to the works of Mlle de Scudéry: "One cannot help but be astonished at what this woman, as illustrious for her modesty as for her talent, has created under an assumed name, thus depriving herself of the glory due her by seeking her recompense only in her virtue: it is as though she worked for the glory of our nation and wanted, at the same time, to avoid shaming those of our sex."[19]

Ménage, too, paid tribute to Mlle de Scudéry the novelist. He emphasized the ties that heroic novels had with the *poème épique* and defended their complexity:

If the epic poem must include a certain number of occurrences in order to suspend the unfolding of a story that deals only with a part of the protagonist's life, it does so because without these events the story would come too rapidly to its conclusion. Without this device one would not experience the pleasure that comes from the type of spectacle that is produced at the end of the novel when most of the subplots are reunited with the principal plot. Mlle de Scudéry has managed this technique so well and has devised so many beautiful pages that, as a result, nothing else in this genre is comparable to what she has done. . . . Mlle de Scudéry has fashioned in our souls the grandest of sentiments that this type of literature should inspire.

Ménage also affirms the heroic novel's superiority over the *nouvelles* "which do not cause one to conceive of anything either useful or majestic."[20]

One can also find words of praise for Mlle de Scudéry coming from rather unexpected sources. Charles Sorel, who was very original on the subject of novels, passed judgement quite favorably on Sapho in his *Bibliothèque françoise*, published in 1664, a time when the heroic novel was already under heavy attack. Sorel himself had written *Les Nouvelles françoises* dating from 1623, but reflecting on the relationship between the epic novel and the *nouvelles*, he wrote: "Since they [the nouvelles] represent only certain superficialities of life instead of establishing real relationships, we must, in order to find a more complete entertainment, be presented with the more ample relationship that one encounters in the heroic novel with its many wonderful adventures." He went on to speak of the "wise and knowledgeable demoiselle" who had written *Cyrus* and *Clélie*, both of which he praised highly.[21]

The importance of Mlle de Scudéry's novels can also be seen by the amount of material that has been borrowed from them. According to Cousin and Brunetière, Molière got the idea for *Le Misanthrope* from *Cyrus*. Despite the publication of Francis Baumal's *Molière, Auteur précieux*, or the articles of Cottez and Whitfield, which study the material that Molière took from Mlle de Scudéry's novels closely, it is still a not very well known subject. These articles deal with much more than *Le Misanthrope*, also citing other works, among which the most obvious are *Les Amants magnifiques*, *Mélicerte*, and *Dom Garcie de Navarre*.[22]

For the modern reader the familiarity that Molière had with Mlle de Scudéry's novels is more obvious in the direct allusions he made rather than in the borrowed material, which is difficult to recognize now because the novels are no longer read. In the words of Marotte, the servant to the heroines of *Les Précieuses ridicules*, the two girls learned the *"filophie dans le Grand Cyre"* (philosophy in *Le Grand Cyrus*), and obviously Molière did too, even if he did put the knowledge to better use! However, the use Molière made of the many allusions to the novels of Mlle de Scudéry should not be misinterpreted. If Cathos and Magdelon, the two *pecques provinciales*, expected to experience in their everyday lives the adventures described throughout Mlle de Scudéry's novels, Molière was poking fun at them for not having understood that it was a novel and therefore not to be taken seriously. This could not have concerned Mlle de Scudéry any more than the vocabulary used in the play, which was not hers. It was much more reminiscent of the style typified by Nervèze and Des Escuteaux, two authors already considered passé during the time of the *Précieuses*.[23] In *Sganarelle ou Le Cocu imaginaire*, Moliére has one of the characters make this criticism of *Clélie:*

> Et vous parlez de Dieu bien moins que de *Clélie*.
> Jetez-moi dans le feu tous ces méchants écrits
> Qui gâtent tous les jours tant de jeunes esprits. (l 31–33)[24]

Gorgibus is chastizing his daughter for speaking about *Clélie* more than of God, and comments that this type of writing was ruining the young people. The seriousness of the statement, however, is negated when he recommends that she read, instead, Pibrac's *Quatrains* or *La Guide des pécheurs*, material of a religious nature that was often handled mockingly by Molière.

In *L'Ecole des maris*, Sganarelle takes the same approach toward the education of a young woman. His brother Ariste, who seems to be expressing Molière's opinion on the matter, wins the love of a young girl by arriving at *Tendre sur Estime*, one of the points on Mlle de Scudéry's *Carte de Tendre* where love comes as a result of trust and respect. He speaks of the *tendre amitié* (verse 1062)[25] that he has always shown the young girl, and therefore seriously utilizes the topography of the imaginary kingdom made popular by Mlle de Scudéry.

If it seems increasingly difficult to include Molière among Mlle de Scudéry's true critics, this is not the case with Furetière. Even though he declared himself to be Sapho's "most humble and obedient of admirers," he scoffed at her choice of celibacy in this witty allusion to her invention of the Kingdom of Tendre: "The Virgin of the Marais has restricted herself to the creation of this world and has left the task of populating it to others" (R, 67). In *Le Roman bourgeois* he made this portrait of Mlle de Scudéry under the name of Polymathie, which, despite the compliments, is dominated by its bantering tone:

Polymathie did not receive her fair share of beauty; her homeliness was of the highest degree, and I would hesitate to describe it fully in fear of offending the sensibility of the more delicate of readers. It is actually not possible for girls to be both knowledgeable and beautiful at the same time because reading until all hours of the night causes them to have dark rings under their eyes. They also are unable to conserve a beautiful complexion and a pleasant roundness if they do not lead a delicate and pampered existence. There is no time for study when the day is already not long enough for them to apply their makeup and to adorn themselves. But on the other hand Polymathie was blessed with incomparable wit, and she spoke so well that one was charmed in listening if not in looking. She knew philosophy and the loftiest of sciences, but she never expressed herself in the pedantic manner of the colleges. Her admirable work in both poetry and prose attracted to her side the most renowned and refined persons of her century.[26]

It is difficult to know if Furetière, a friend of Gilles Boileau, was writing negatively of the woman who was bitterly opposed to Boileau, or of the novelist. Sapho was very firm in her opinions and sometimes aroused anger, but it was anger directed at the woman, not the author. This was the case of Godeau, who was temporarily not on speaking terms with her, and in a letter to Mme de Rambouillet referred to her as that "scribbler."[27] However, they were reconciled only a few months later. Balzac, too, had this to say of Mlle de Scudéry in a letter to Chapelain: "This woman has the nature of a wasp that pesters you whether you chase it or not."[28]

The correspondence between Balzac and Chapelain has a great many of the bittersweet remarks in regard to "the Muse of the Marais." Both adopted a patronizing tone, but both acknowledged her merits. It seems that the efforts of Mlle de Scudéry to establish a correspondence with personages such as Balzac and Chapelain had the effect of annoying them in the process. In their correspondence they mockingly referred to Mlle de Scudéry as *La Pucelle*, but their criticism was in regard to her personality. Nevertheless, Chapelain was known in later years, when Mlle de Scudéry's career as a novelist was well established, to have praised her work. In a letter in which he gave his opinion on novels he said that the form was invented by the French "four hundred years ago." He ranked d'Urfé as the greatest of modern novelists, and divided second place among Desmarets de Saint-Sorlin, La Calprenède, and Mlle de Scudéry.

B. *Boileau*

When one studies what Boileau wrote in regard to Mlle de Scudéry, the opposite situation is presented. He seems to have had a great deal of respect for the woman, but attacked her works for reasons clearly spelled out.

It has been suggested that the dispute that arose over Gilles Boileau's election to the *Académie française* in 1659 played a role in the attitude his brother adopted in regard to Mlle de Scudéry's novels. This is not to be ruled out, but it is known that relations between Nicolas and Gilles Boileau were frequently not of the best, and Nicolas certainly did not always take part in the disputes involving his older brother.[29] Furthermore, Nicolas Boileau and Pellisson both attended President Lamoignon's *Lundis*, and this leads one to suppose that their relationship was a civil one. According to Brossette, the first version of *Satire VIII* contained this line: "L'or même à Pellisson donne un teint de beauté" (Gold makes even Pellisson look good). But this was changed in the published version to "Gold makes even ugliness look good," and this certainly was more acceptable to the sensitive and stubborn Acante.

More than likely Nicolas Boileau's attack on Mlle de Scudéry's work was not prompted by a clannish dispute, but rather by opposition to her concept of the novel. His criticisms were numerous and took various forms. Sometimes they were merely in the form of unpleasant allusions, such as in *Satire III*,[30] or as in the fifth canto of *Le Lutrin*[31] where he makes scornful references to "the horrible

Artamène" and to Clélie, that "woman so calamitous for more than one warrior." These allusions, referred to by Mlle de Scudéry as Boileau's "usual barbs," annoyed her but did not seem to draw blood.

With the *Satire X*, however, Boileau's criticism began to cut more deeply. In this antifeminist work he mocked knowledgeable women, and he intentionally lumped them together with the pedantic women that had been ridiculed by Molière. He said that they associated with the supporters of the *faux bel esprit* and for them "all poetry was beautiful as long as it was new." This attack on the *modernes*, however, was not the only criticism. What hurt Mlle de Scudéry the most was the accusation that her writings fostered immorality. The *Satire X* is a letter from Boileau to Alcippe, a young man about to marry, and he warned him in this way about his future wife:

> D'abord tu la verras ainsi que dans *Clélie*
> Recevant ses amants sous le doux nom d'amis
> S'en tenir avec eux aux petits soins permis:
> Puis bientôt en grande eau sur le fleuve de Tendre
> Naviguer à souhait. . . .[32]

(At first you will see her, as they do in *Clélie*, receiving her lovers under the sweet guise of friendship, being as solicitous as is permitted; but soon she will leave the river Tendre to navigate in more dangerous waters.) Mlle de Scudéry took great offense at this accusation and made allusions to it several times in her correspondence. For example, in a letter to Abbé Boisot she wrote: "He [Boileau] has such a bad opinion of women that he can count only three honest ones in all of Paris. But while he believes this work [*Satire X*] to be his masterpiece, the public finds it quite *bourgeois* and filled with rather uncivilized phrases" (R, 371). It is ironic that Mlle de Scudéry, employing what she considered to be the supreme insult, accused Boileau of being a *bourgeois*, and that he, in turn, accused her of the very same fault. His accusation of immorality, however, is not to be taken lightly, and in his *Dialogue des Héros de roman* he explained his position toward Mlle de Scudéry's novels in detailed fashion.

At first he confessed that he, like everyone else, enjoyed her novels as well as those by La Calprenède, and regarded them as masterpieces of the French language. However, with the passing of time, and as a result of reflection, he became increasingly aware of the genre's weaknesses. He composed his *Dialogue*, but did not publish it because he did not wish to risk offending Mlle de Scudéry, whom he respected: "Her intelligence is exceeded only by her integrity and her honor."[33]

His criticisms, therefore, were not directed at Sapho, "despite the bad morals taught in her novels," but at the genre itself, which she so eminently represented. As a matter of fact, this particular criticism was often used by moralists to point out that the novel was a literary form of little value. Arnauld wrote a letter to Perrault, printed in the beginning of the 1701 edition of *Satire X*, that brilliantly developed this theme. He wrote this in regard to *Clélie:*

The esteem that one has always had for this work, and the extreme respect one has always had for this illustrious author, have caused everyone to rise against an attack so often and so uselessly repeated. It is not a question of the author's merit or of the high opinion in which this novel is held. It has earned this as a result of its wit, its urbanity, its charming construction, its well-portrayed characters, and for all the other elements that have made its reading so pleasant for the many devotees of novels. It is, if you wish, the best of novels, but it is, after all, only a novel. Its underlying character is based on love, and it gives lessons in this area of an ingenious sort.[34]

As a result of these seductive lessons, according to Boileau and Arnauld, a young girl would let herself fall into a dangerous situation without being aware of it, so persuasive were the smooth-tongued ideas set forth in the novel.

Yet Mlle de Scudéry answered this accusation in advance by having one of the characters in *Clélie* state: "Love is not learned from novels at all. It is nature that teaches mankind about love and it does so everywhere" (VIII, 1143). She believed, furthermore, that love without civility was brutal and coarse, and it was this very civility she expounded upon in her novels. Mlle de Scudéry also clearly pointed out that women could not be led to licentious behavior as a result of having read her work because: "If they wanted to make a comparison between the love they have in real life and the love depicted in a book of that nature, they would find so great a difference that they would not allow themselves to indulge in such a relationship" (VIII, 1145–46).

This idea was taken up by La Bruyère in *Les Caractères*. The chapter "Des Ouvrages de l'esprit" referred to novels as well as to plays. He commented: "One sees in them such grand examples of constancy, virtue, tenderness, unselfishness, and characters of such beauty and perfection that when a young girl looks away from the novels and finds herself surrounded by persons of little worth, and certainly much below the level of the characters she had come to admire in novels, I would be astonished if she were then capable of feeling the slightest sympathy for these individuals."[35] In his eulogy of Mlle de Scudéry, Bosquillon went even further. He saw the examples set forth in novels as models of virtue that were difficult, if not impossible, for ordinary persons to emulate: "It is a school for the development of *honnêtes gens,* where the heart and the mind, far from being in danger of corruption, run no risk other than being unable to attain the height and perfection of the models set before them."[36]

The moral aspect, however, is but one of the points under attack by Boileau. He also criticized Mlle de Scudéry's works for "their lack of solidity, for their affectations, for their vague and frivolous conversations, for their repeatedly flattering portraits of persons of mediocre beauty, even sometimes of an excessive ugliness, and for their unending and verbose passages of love"[37] (*Dialogue* 445).

Another crime, probably less pardonable in the eyes of this partisan of the *Anciens,* was the erroneous use of history to suit the needs of the novel. The *Dialogue* achieves one of its truly comical moments when it juxtaposes the fierce Cyrus "who had won so many battles" in which thirty to forty thousand men were slain each day, with the Cyrus who, languidly leaning upon his squire, complains in dying tones of the severity of his unfeeling Mandane.

In the third canto of *L'Art poétique,* Boileau, in one of his condensed and unforgettable phrases, made this reproach: "N'allez pas d'un Cyrus nous faire un Artamène" ("Don't make of Cyrus an Artamène"), thus referring to the fact that Cyrus, represented in the novel as Artamène, is shown mainly pursuing the hand of Mandane, the primary motivation for all of his exploits. As for *Clélie,* he made this comment:

> Gardez-vous de donner ainsi que dans *Clélie*
> L'air ni l'esprit français à l'antique Italie,
> Et sous des noms romains faisant votre portrait
> Peindre Caton galant et Brutus dameret.[38]

(Don't attribute to ancient Italy, as is done in *Clélie,* the air and spirit of France, and even though you portray yourselves under Roman names, don't make of Cato a gallant and of Brutus a fop.) Carried away with the comical image of Cato the Censor being portrayed as a lover, Boileau himself was guilty of an anachronism. The story of the novel took place in the sixth century B.C., at a time when Cato did not exist.[39] The problem, however, was clearly expressed. Boileau wanted history to be authentically depicted, and this included the personages and customs. Mlle de Scudéry, as it is well documented, could have easily made her work historically correct if she had so desired, but she felt that this was not at all a novelist's objective.

In *Clélie* she approached the problem numerous times and clearly expressed her beliefs. She felt that after having selected a century that was known, but not too close to cause the reader to be shocked by fictitious events, the author was obliged to respect a certain number of principles. She enumerated them in this way: "One should take the trouble to study well the century that one has chosen in order to profit from all that is unusual. One should restrict the customs to the place that is written about and should not have plants grow where they have never been seen. One also should not mix centuries in regard to customs or religions, although one can, using good judgement, accommodate the facts somewhat to correspond more to our century in order to be more pleasing to the reader" (*Clélie,* VIII, 1135–36).

In this she was in agreement with many writers of the time, and in *De La Lecture des vieux romans,* which Chapelain wrote in 1647, he stated: "I submit that writers who invent a story in which the subject revolves around human action should have their characters conform to the customs and the beliefs of the writer's own century."[40]

In writing *Clélie,* Mlle de Scudéry read her sources with great care, and she retained enough information to be able to create an effect of local color. She also added all sorts of anachronisms that pleased her readers but that greatly angered Boileau. The main rule she adhered to was one of plausibility. Even if the history of Brutus or Horatius is not as depicted in the novel, it was not altogether impossible. One of the characters in *Clélie,* judging a story of this type, made these comments in regard to the author, which surely reflect Mlle de Scudéry's opinion: "He has profited rather well from what history has given him, and I found myself disposed to believe that if it was not as he depicted it, it very well could have been. There is no doubt that nothing helps to establish a story better than an historical basis which runs throughout the story and with which it becomes easier to mix invention with truth" (VIII, 1124–25).

There is, then, a profound difference between what Mlle de Scudéry and Boileau considered plausible. For example, since Horatius was a man it was not impossible for him to be in love with Clélie, an historical contemporary. Starting with that possibility, Mlle de Scudéry constructed a story in which this love was the motivation for all of Horatius' historically documented exploits. For Boileau, as well as for modern readers, this mixture of one portion of historical fact with nine of anachronism—that is to say the attribution of *attitudes précieuses* to Horatius—seems difficult to accept. It was, however, a convention that assuredly did not shock readers of the seventeenth century, or at least not until the 1660s.


C. *The evolution of taste after 1660*

Rather than establishing a new mode, Boileau, in his criticism of Mlle de Scudéry's novels, seems to have been following the taste of the time. Instead of forcing the old conventions to disappear, the change in taste seems merely to have altered them in such a way as to make them more acceptable. This is attributed to the appearance of the *nouvelle*.[41] Its major characteristics were, of course, to shorten the text considerably, to make an attempt at greater plausibility, and to place the story closer to the author's time. The ten volume novel seemed to lose its popularity among writers, and it was this, rather than a supposed attack by Molière, that caused a change in Mlle de Scudéry's style.

Segrais, with his *Nouvelles françoises* of 1656, as well as Mme de Lafayette with *La Princesse de Montpensier* in 1662, or Mme de Villedieu with *Lysandre* in 1663,[42] used some of the ideas put forth by Sorel at the beginning of the century to brilliantly represent the new genre. Pizzorusso has pointed out that Mlle de Scudéry was quite sensitive to the evolution of taste regarding the novel,[43] and that she conformed to it accordingly. *Clélie* was her last novel of ample proportions, and as early as 1661 she published *Célinte, Nouvelle première*, which followed the format of the new style, as did her *Mathilde d'Aguilar*, published in 1667, and *Célanire* in 1669. In her volumes of *Conversations* she included a few *nouvelles*, or *histoires*, such as "Les Bains des Thermopyles" in 1680, and "L'Histoire du Comte d'Albe" in 1685.

It should be noted, however, that certain conventions of the epic novel did not completely disappear and were found, somewhat modified, in many *nouvelles* and *histoires*. *La Princesse de Clèves*, for example, does not truly depict the court of Henry II, but describes instead the court of Louis XIV. The closeness in time, which is not more than a century of difference, makes the assimilation much easier. It was, in effect, less surprising to have a man of the sixteenth century speak and behave like a man of the seventeenth century, than to have the founders of the Roman Republic sighing for love in the salons of the *Précieuses*.

Another of Mme de Lafayette's devices was to use historical personages of secondary importance, or to invent them altogether. The Prince de Clèves, for example, did exist, but little is known of him; and Mme de Chartres, as well as her daughter, were Mme de Lafayette's own creations. The important figures of history, such as Mary Stuart, were used in an episodic fashion and did not run contrary to what was known of them historically. In such a way, historical facts and personages formed a framework in which the author's creations could freely evolve. This technique, then, was quite different from Mlle de Scudéry's method of selecting as her heroes the great names of Roman history. The great distance in time and the fact that she used Rome as the setting made the anachronisms much more evident.

Although an author of *nouvelles*, Mme de Villedieu stayed rather close to Mlle de Scudéry's novelistic principles in regard to the use of well-known historical figures. In the notice to the reader of her *Les Désordres de l'amour* she justified the "modification of historical events" with these words: "One inserts historical personages in order to gratify more pleasantly the imagination."[44] In the first part of the *nouvelle*, she explained the important role that love played in motivating the characters: "Love is the motive for all the passions of the soul and . . . if one carefully examined the secret reasons for the revolutions of monarchies one would find that love was always the cause or the accomplice."

We see then that the change in taste that came about in regard to the novel was not a radical one. It surely affected the length, which was considerably shortened, and the historical period, which was much closer to the author's own era, but a number of ingredients that made the epic novel so successful were not basically changed.

## II  *After the Seventeenth Century*

It is necessary, in fact, not to exaggerate the effect of this new movement. When M. Godenne writes that "the novel of the period 1615–1650, after having known a prodigious success, at last became tiresome and disappeared from the literary scene for more than fifty years,"[45] it was more a question of their not being written rather than of their not being read. As Georges May has noted,[46] readers remained faithful to the old genre for many years to come, and regardless of the numerous assurances that the day of the long novel had passed, Mlle de Scudéry's books were read until the end of the eighteenth century.

In 1731 the *Mercure* announced a new edition of Mlle de Scudéry's novels, adding: "All the admirers of civility and heroic gallantry can rejoice in these books."[47] In the *Bibliothèque des romans*, a work which summarized the plots of great novels, a large portion was dedicated to Mlle de Scudéry's works. Readers, therefore, continued to be interested in her works, and M. Mongrédien has mentioned that a handwritten copy of *Les Femmes illustres* with Marie-Antoinette's coat of arms was prepared between the years 1772 and 1775. Rousseau, in *Les Confessions*, wrote of having read *Cyrus* in his youth,[48] and we have learned in *Les Mémoires d'Outre-Tombe*[49] that Chateaubriand's mother was supposed to have known the novel by heart.

In his *Dictionnaire*,[50] Bayle paid hommage to Mlle de Scudéry by stating that she wrote perfectly well in both prose and poetry. Abbé Prévost, in *Le Pour et le contre*, wrote sympathetically of Mlle de Scudéry and the epic novel. Far from criticizing "these pleasant fantasies of the human spirit," he accuses the reader of his time of being in too much of a hurry to appreciate the heroic novel. He further commented that his contemporaries were barely capable of finishing "little stories" and seemed to enjoy only the conclusion of a novel![51]

This attitude represented by Prévost was, however, becoming increasingly rare, and critiques, mainly from specialists of literary history, were multiplying by leaps and bounds. Voltaire, in *Le Siècle de Louis XIV,*[52] praised Mlle de Scudéry's poetry and considered it far superior to her "enormous novels." We see, however, in a letter to Mme du Deffand, that he had a copy of *Clélie* in his library at Ferney, and he commented that "it was more interesting than one would think." He was especially interested in the portraits Mlle de Scudéry drew of her contemporaries.[53] Marmontel in his *Essai sur les romans* was extremely severe in his criticisms of La Calprenède, but was even more so in regard to Mlle de Scudéry: "The middle class civility and manners that Mlle de Scudéry lent her insipid heroes, their tasteless and dull gallantry, the indifference of their relationships, the length and monotony of their tortuous sentences, were more disgusting than the contemptible long-windedness of the Gascon novelist."[54]

The Chevalier de Jaucourt's article on novels, which appeared in *L'Encyclopédie,* followed quite closely the opinion set forth by Boileau. In fact, this became the prevalent position regarding criticisms of Mlle de Scudéry's novels. La Harpe admitted in his *Lycée ou Cours de littérature:* "I have not been able to finish either *Cyrus* or *Clélie,* which Boileau quite correctly ridiculed."[55] That authors criticizing these novels did not read them is confirmed by the fact that they even copied one another in citing the approximate number of pages contained in *Clélie* or *Cyrus.*

Despite Victor Cousin's attempt in the nineteenth century, with his *La Sociéte française au XVIIème siècle d'après Le Grand Cyrus,* to rehabilitate at least this novel, there was a well-established current running through critiques of Mlle de Scudéry's works that meant to relegate them to absolute oblivion. It is to be noted that Cousin himself was quite harsh in his criticism of *Clélie:* "In *Clélie* Mlle de Scudéry, instead of portraying contemporary high society, chose to describe her own society; that is to say a society quite inferior and middle class, incessantly occupied in petty gallantry, insipid poetry, and wit of a lower order."[56]

If Cousin, who championed Mlle de Scudéry for her *Cyrus,* chose to write so disparagingly of *Clélie,* it is not surprising that favorable comments upon her novels were pitifully rare in the nineteenth century. Although an author like Edouard de Barthélémy wrote that "Mlle de Scudéry has been perhaps the most accomplished of the intelligent and informed *Précieuses,*" and "perhaps the most original representative of the seventeenth century,"[57] most critics, such as Sainte-Beuve, who paid homage to her wit and her qualities as a governess, unanimously declared her novels to be unreadable.[58] Saint-Marc Girardin in his *Cours de littérature*[59] displayed originality in a chapter dedicated to a serious analysis of *Clélie*, but Faguet expressed the opinion too often accepted today when he wrote: "Mlle de Scudéry was a true *Précieuse ridicule,* one of those that Molière and all the classic school alluded to."[60]

The unfortunate association that Mlle de Scudéry has allegedly had with *Les Précieuses ridicules* remains firmly entrenched today despite some excellent works that clearly establish that this theory, though tempting, is a false one. Furthermore, Adam has pointed out that the reading of Mlle de Scudéry's works is indispensable for the comprehension of that phenomenon known as *Préciosité.*

## III Foreign Acclaim

In André Bellessort's *Heures de parole*[61] it is clearly indicated that Mlle de Scudéry was "a European novelist." She undoubtedly played as important a role in the dissemination of French culture as many of the great classics. Convinced as many are today of her downgraded esteem, it is easy to forget the international success her works once enjoyed. She herself, stepping out of her usually modest posture, made this comment in a letter to Abbé Boisot in 1694 on Boileau's attack in regard to *Clélie:* "A book that has been translated into Italian, English, German, and Arabic can well do without the praises of a writer of his sort" (R, 370). A bibliography of Mlle de Scudéry's works compiled by Georges Mongrédien shows that she neglected to mention a Spanish translation made in 1692.

A rapid glance is sufficient to observe that her fame was equally great and durable outside of her own country. Her election to the Academy of the Ricovrati clearly establishes that she was both well known and highly appreciated in the Italian scholarly world, but her renown was far from limited to Italy. Her glory seems to have also been well founded in England, where translations of *Ibrahim, Cyrus, Clélie,* and several volumes of the *Conversations* had numerous readers. In *The Spectator* of Thursday, April 12, 1711, Addison described a "Lady's Library" where one found *Le Grand Cyrus* "with a pen stuck in one of the middle leaves," as well as *Clélie* "which opened of itself in the place that describes two lovers in a bower."[62] In Pepy's *Diary* his wife appears as a great reader of Mlle de Scudéry. She would read *Cyrus* until midnight, and once embarrassed her husband during a voyage in recounting *Le Grand Cyrus* "though nothing to the purpose nor in any good manner."[63] Despite this incident, he purchased *Ibrahim* for her. When she attended a performance of Dryden's *Evening's Love or the Mock Astrologer*, which he admitted contained "a little" material borrowed from *Ibrahim*, she commented that the entire play had been taken from the novel.

Steele's play *The Tender Husband* also made numerous allusions to Mlle de Scudéry and her novels, which were the favorite reading material of the heroine Biddy Tipkin. The direct references to Mlle de Scudéry's works indicate that the public had an excellent knowledge of them. Another character in the play said, for example, "Your case is exactly the same with the Princess of the Leontines in *Clelia*."[64] The author was not even mentioned, because it was clearly unnecessary—everyone knew who it was. Sir Walter Scott in *The Life of John Dryden* also testified to the popularity of La Calprenède and de Scudéry despite their length and their defects.[65]

Mlle de Scudéry's fame among the English was such that when Martin Lister traveled to Paris at the end of the seventeenth century he included her name as one of the celebrities to visit. His disappointment upon meeting her could not have been greater, because he had surely imagined her as she was in her younger days: "Amongst the persons of distinction and fame, I was desirous to see Madamoiselle de Scudéry, now 91 years of age. Her mind is yet vigorous, tho' her body is in ruins. I confess this visit was a perfect mortification, to see the sad decays of Nature in a woman once so famous."[66]

Even if she somewhat facetiously doubted that "German was truly a language after listening to the harsh jargon of the Swiss Guard or Swiss hotel employees" (R, 195), Mlle de Scudéry had many readers and admirers in that country. Leibnitz, for example, was considered to be one of her friends and spoke of her with respect. In the dispute he had over divine love with Bossuet and Fénelon, he called upon the judgement of women to settle the question, but insisted upon women "that resemble Mlle de Scudéry, who clarified so well the characters and passions in her novels and in her conversations on morals" (R, 129).

Wagenseil, a native of Nüremberg, visited Paris in 1664, and while there went to call on Mlle de Scudéry. He has left a lengthy account of his stay and of his meeting with the renowned French novelist. He found himself in the capital at a time when a band of thieves was robbing those on the streets at night. A letter of protest in poetic form was written to the king in the name of the lovers who could not go out at night in order to court their beloveds, and Mlle de Scudéry, in turn, responded to this letter in the name of the thieves: "Un amant qui craint les voleurs/Ne mérite pas de faveurs" (R, 514). (A lover who fears thieves does not deserve a woman's favors.) This episode was described in detail by Wagenseil, and it ultimately served as the inspiration for Hoffmann's *Das Fräulein Von Scuderi*.[67] Although he mixed a number of anachronisms to make the tale more attractive, this seems to indicate that Mlle de Scudéry had not been forgotten in Germany, even a century after her death.

Hopefully, this brief panorama has clearly demonstrated the importance of Mlle de Scudéry's role in the literature of her time. Despite the change in literary style and the severe criticisms of the epic novel, her fame continued for nearly a century. Thereafter her name all but disappeared, buried under the years that followed. It must be remembered, however, that the criticisms of her work came only after a period of brilliant acclaim, and they cannot begin to counterbalance the glory she knew.

CHAPTER 6

# *Conclusion*

A FTER one has become truly acquainted with the works of Mlle
de Scudéry, it is frustrating to note the condescending smile
that just the mention of her name evokes. The identical criticisms
and often repeated quotations, strangely similar to those found in
Victor Cousin's *La Société française d'après Le Grand Cyrus*, are
evidence that the modern opinion of Mlle de Scudéry is based
mainly on hearsay and not on a critical study of her works themselves. The truth of the matter is that few people since the seventeenth century have actually read Mlle de Scudéry's works with any
thoroughness, and that she has been forgotten for reasons that are,
for the most part, due to a complete change in reading taste.

Her books are undeniably long, and they were written for a society that had certain rules of which we have little understanding or
appreciation today. The complicated plots and subplots, the detailed discussions on love, and the lack of precision in the descriptions of persons and everyday life bother us today. But this is a
general problem that one encounters when approaching most
seventeenth century works.

Nevertheless, it is a fact that Mlle de Scudéry has left us the only
precise description of the *société précieuse*, even though she herself
never used this terminology. One need not look into the works of
Abbé de Pure or Somaize to have an idea of this society. These
authors were often guilty of a rather ambiguous attitude toward the
*Précieuses*, and their frequent lack of sincerity has resulted in giving the modern reader a false impression. In Mlle de Scudéry we
have a more accurate representation of her world.

This is a limited world of *honnêtes gens*, where material and
physical needs are nonexistent, where everyone is of the same culture and has the same passion for conversation and diversion. Contrary to customary belief, the *Précieux* did not take themselves seri-

156

ously and were certainly not a group of boring fuddyduddies. Above all, theirs was a world in which a good sense of humor was an absolute necessity.

Since women enjoyed a position of preeminence in this society, they were depicted as such by Mlle de Scudéry, who devoted a great amount of time to the study of feminine psychology. Cousin correctly considered her to be the founder of the psychological novel because of her detailed studies of love and women.

Despite the rise of pessimism in the latter part of the seventeenth century, Mlle de Scudéry continued to be inspired by her *joie de vivre,* and if she mentioned the theory of *"refus,"* it was only to discard it. Until the end of her long stay on earth she loved life and her role in it, and she was able to avoid the "inexorable boredom" that beset Mme de Lafayette or Mme de Maintenon. This love for life is one of Mlle de Scudéry's most attractive qualities, to be sure, but when one comes to the full realization that she was one of the most knowledgeable women in French history, and the most acclaimed novelist of her time, the attitude of condescension quickly turns into one of respect and admiration.

# Notes and References

Place of publication is Paris unless otherwise noted.

## Chapter One

1. Tallemant des Réaux, *Historiettes,* ed. Antoine Adam (Pléiade, 1961), II, 685.
2. Rathery et Boutron, *Mademoiselle de Scudéry; Sa vie et sa correspondance* (Téchener, 1873), p. 3. The quotations from this book will be indicated in the text by the letter R. Georges de Scudéry's marriage contract in 1599 still included both names: Scudéry or Lescuyer. According to Charles Livet, *Précieux et Précieuses* (Waelter, 1895), p. 211, Nicéron in his *Mémoires pour servir à l'histoire des hommes illustres de l République des Lettres.* XVI, indicated that the name Scudéry came from the Latin Scutifer and that this eventually led to the French version Scudier-Escuyer.
3. Charles Clerc, *Un Matamore des Lettres: La Vie tragic-omique de Georges de Scudéry* (SPES, 1929), p. 35.
4. Zobeidah Youssef, *Polémique et littérature chez Guez de Balzac* (Nizet, 1971), p. 181, note 54. See also Clerc, pp. 130–32. During the dispute over *Le Cid* a conciliatory statement appeared in which it was said: "*Le Cid* derives no shame in being ranked with this masterpiece *(L'Amour tyrannique)* of Georges de Scudéry." In his "Bibliographie des Oeuvres de Georges et Madeleine de Scudéry," printed in *La Revue d'Histoire Littéraire de la France,* 40 (1933), Georges Mongrédien cites some figures that show the considerable success of Georges de Scudéry's works in the seventeenth century. *Alaric* and *La Mort de César* were reprinted six times. This demonstrates a great commercial success when one considers that during Corneille's lifetime *Le Cid* was reprinted eight times and *Polyeucte* six times. *Andromaque* had only three editions and *Phèdre,* four, during Racine's lifetime. For further details on Georges de Scudéry's military

159

career see, besides Clerc, Antoine Adam's notes in his edition of Tallemant des Réaux *Historiettes*, mainly, II, 1453.

5. Mongrédien, p. 558.

6. Tallemant, II, 688.

7. Tallemant, II, 689.

8. Victor Cousin, *La Société française au XVIIème siècle d'après Le Grand Cyrus* (Perrin, 1905), I, 53. Regarding the battles, Thybarra describes the battle of Lens; the battle against the Massagetae is a depiction of Rocroy; and the siege of Cumae actually represents the siege of Dunkerque. As to the publication of the secret documents of the Condé library in the eighteenth century see page 139.

9. Tallemant, *Historiettes*, II, 693.

10. Boileau, *Dialogue des Héros de roman*, in *Oeuvres complètes*, ed. F. Escal, (Pléiade, 1966), p. 445.

11. Emile Magne, *Le Coeur et l'esprit de Mme de Lafayette* (Emile-Paul Frères, 1927), p. 52.

12. Clerc, p. 116. In the preface to *Le Cabinet de Mr de Scudéry* (Courbé, 1646), Georges de Scudéry describes "so many beautiful things that I have either seen or have owned."

13. Loret in *La Muse historique*, ed. Livet (Daffis, 1877–1878), III, 451, indicates that Mlle de Scudéry received a pension and a diamond worth seven hundred pistoles. In December 1663, he mentions a gift from the king of four hundred écus. Rathery and Boutron (p. 109) indicate the pension given by Mazarin. Mme de Sévigné, *Lettres*, ed. Gérard-Gailly (Pléiade, 1960), II, 929 (March 5, 1683) mentions another royal pension. See Bosquillon, "Eloge de Mlle de Scudéry," *Journal des Savants* (July 11, 1701), p. 319; and Jacques Wilhem, *La Vie quotidienne au Marais au XVIIème* (Hachette, 1966), p. 198. There are, however, various references to the difficulty Mlle de Scudéry had, at times, in obtaining the payment of her pensions, R. 110, and Paul Scarron, *Epître chagrine à Mlle de Scudéry*, in *Poésies diverses*, ed. Maurice Cauche (Didier, 1961), II, 256–58.

14. Antoine Adam, "La Préciosité," *Cahiers de l'Association des Etudes françaises*, I (1959), 39.

15. Claude Aragonnès, *Madeleine de Scudéry, Reine du Tendre* (Colin, 1934), p. 13. The "Bulletins de Clément" give November 15, 1607, as her birthdate (R. 4).

16. Conrart was Théodamas in *Cyrus*, and his house in Athis-sur-Mons was known as Carisatis in *Clélie*. Conrart often referred to his wife as "La Maîtresse de Carisatis," R. Kerviler and E. de Barthélémy, *Valentin Conrart, sa vie et sa correspondance* (Didier, 1881), p. 579; Mongrédien, *Madeleine de Scudéry et son salon*, (Tallandier, 1946), pp. 71–75. As for the madrigals they exchanged see, E. Colombey, *La Journée des madrigaux* (Aubry, 1856), pp. 39–42. In regard to the exchange of poems between

Conrart and Mlle de Scudéry, it must be remembered that this was considered to be part of the *vie de salon*. Furthermore, Conrart's wife was always present at the receptions in Paris, and it was she who received at Athis-sur-Mons. In reality the three of them were considered to be excellent friends, Kerviler and de Barthélémy, p. 74.

17. L. Monmerqué, *Mémoires de Valentin Conrart* (Paris, 1826; rpt. Geneva: Slatkine, 1971), pp. 253–56. Clerc (p. 30), has the mother live until 1635, but he does not give the source of this information. It can be noted, however, that Tallemant mentions (II, 686), that Mlle de Scudéry read novels when she was quite young, and that her confessor told her mother that this would not have a bad effect on her. Since Mme de Scudéry died in 1613, when her daughter was only six years old, it is difficult to believe, even allowing for a certain precocity, that she was reading novels at such a tender age. The story, however, could well have been true and would lose nothing in credibility if the priest had said this to Mlle de Scudéry's uncle, or to her aunt.

18. Tallemant, II, 685–86.

19. E. Gérard-Gailly, *Madame de Sévigné* (Hachette, 1971), p. 27. Dorothy McDougall, *Madeleine de Scudéry, Her Romantic Life and Death* (London, 1938), p. 47, also makes reference to Mlle de Scudéry's spirit and gaiety.

20. The only notable exception is Elise's mother, Barcé, who persecuted her daughter in *Cyrus*. This story recounts Mlle Paulet's life and depicts her true relationship with her mother, Cousin, I, 283.

21. Letter of April 21, 1639, cited in Youssef, p. 188.

22. Dorothy Backer, *Precious Women* (New York: Basic Books, 1974), p. 65.

23. Antoine Adam, *Histoire de la littérature française au XVIIème siècle* (Del Duca, 1958) I, 265. Emile Magne, *Voiture et les origines de l'Hôtel de Rambouillet* (Mercure de France, 1911), pp. 100 and 118.

24. Magne, pp. 115–17 and 211.

25. Magne, pp. 125–33.

26. Magne, p. 100.

27. A. Ubicini, *Oeuvres de Voiture* (Paris, 1855; rpt. Geneva: Slatkine, 1967), II, 292, 296, and 303. Magne, *Voiture et les années de gloire de l'Hôtel de Rambouillet: 1635–1638* (Emile-Paul, 1930), pp. 38–39.

28. Jean Rousset, "Les difficultés de l'autoportrait," *Revue d'Histoire Littéraire de la France* (mai-août 1969), p. 541.

29. Tallemant, II, 689.

30. In his edition of Tallemant Adam gives Chapelain's letter in a note, II, 1453.

31. Paul Festugière, *Oeuvres de J. Fr. Sarasin* (Champion, 1926), I, 108.

32. M. Magendie, *La Politesse mondaine et les théories de l'honnêteté en*

*France, au XVIIème, de 1600 à 1660* (Alcan, 1925), p. 127. About *I Suppositi*, see Youssef, pp. 188–211. Besides the prologue, Mlle de Rambouillet could also have been offended by Act I, scene 1, 99–101; II, 4, 732–34; or even more by V, 12, 1273–74. See Ariosto, *I Suppositi*, ed. Michele Catalano (Bologna: Zanichelli, 1940).

33. Quoted in Youssef, p. 195.

34. Mongrédien, *Madeleine de Scudéry*, pp. 31–41.

35. Emile Perrier, *Scudéry et sa soeur à Marseille* (Valence: Imprimerie Valentinoise, 1908), pp. 26–28.

36. B. Gonot, *Mémoires de Fléchier sur les Grands-Jours tenus à Clermont en 1665–1666* (Porquet, 1844), pp. 63–65.

37. Bernard Pingaud, *Mme de Lafayette par elle-même* (Seuil, 1968), p. 6, names Marc Pioche de la Vergne among Mlle de Scudéry's friends. Emile Magne, *Mme de Lafayette en ménage* (Emile-Paul, 1926), p. 35, indicates that it was he who tried to obtain the position for Mlle de Scudéry. Also see Rathery, p. 421.

38. G. Mongrédien, *Le XVIIème siècle galant: Libertins et amoureuses* (Perrin, 1929), p. 271. In *Polémique et littérature*, Youssef dedicates a section to "Balzac et la querelle des sonnets" where she analyzes Balzac's statement, pp. 220–59.

39. Corneille, *Oeuvres complètes*, ed. A. Stegmann (Seuil, coll. l'Intégrale, 1963), p. 877, "Sonnet sur la contestation entre le sonnet d'Uranie et celui de Job" and "Deux sonnets partagent la ville," and E. Magne, *Mme de la Suze et la société précieuse* (Mercure de France, 1908), p. 61.

40. Jerome Schweitzer in *Georges de Scudéry's Almahide: Authorship, Sources and Structure* (Baltimore: The Johns Hopkins Press, 1939), has established that Mlle de Scudéry had no part in the writing of this novel, p. 215.

41. Somaize, *Le Grand Dictionnaire des Prétieuses* (Paris, 1661; rpt. Geneva: Slatkine, 1972), II, 131.

42. *Ménagiana* (Delaulne, 1693), p. 419.

43. Clerc, p. 52.

44. Wilhem, p. 197.

45. Gustave Charlier, "La Fin de l'Hôtel de Rambouillet," *Revue Belge de Philosophie et d'Histoire*, 18 (1939), 409–26.

46. Loret, III, 516.

47. Emile Magne, *Le Salon de Mlle de Scudéry ou le Royaume de Tendre* (Monaco, 1927), p. 16.

48. Adam, *Histoire de la littérature française au XVIIème siècle*, II, 26–52; Colombey, pp. 10–11.

49. F. L. Marcou, *Etude sur la vie et les oeuvres de Pellisson, suivie d'une correspondance inédite du même* (Didier, 1859), p. 99.

50. Mongrédien, *Madeleine de Scudéry*, p. 115.

51. Colombey, p. 73.

52. Louis Belmont, "Documents inédits sur la société et la littérature précieuses: extraits de la chronique du samedi, publiés d'après le registre original de Pellisson (1652–1657)," *Revue d'histoire littéraire de la France*, 9 (1902), 650.

53. E. Magne, *Voiture et l'Hôtel de Rambouillet: Les Années de gloire, 1635–1648*, p. 185.

54. Colombey, pp. 17–18.

55. Festugière, I, 58.

56. Marcou, p. 136.

57. Mongrédien, *Madeleine de Scudéry*, pp. 103–105.

58. Edouard de Barthélémy, *Sapho, le mage de Sidon et Zénocrate, étude sur la société précieuse d'après des lettres inédites de Mademoiselle de Scudéry, de Godeau et d'Isarn* (Didier, 1880), p. 118.

59. Tallemant, I, 577; the three poems are included in Adam's notes, p. 1187. Cousin, II, pp. 183–85, gives details on the dispute, as does E. Magne, in *Mme de Lafayette en ménage*, p. 177.

60. Marcou, pp. 140 and 306; Adam, *Histoire de la littérature*, II, 174–81; Tallemant, I, note pp. 1185–86. Georges Collas, *Un Poète protecteur des Lettres au XVIIème siècle: Jean Chapelain*, (Picard, 1912), pp. 306–18.

61. Marcou, p. 65.

62. Colombey, p. 80.

63. Belmont, p. 673.

64. Mme de Sévigné, I, 671.

65. According to Abbé d'Olivet, in Belmont, p. 649.

66. Belmont, p. 653.

67. U. V. Chatelain, *Le Surintendant Nicolas Foucquet, Protecteur des Lettres, des Arts et des Sciences* (Perrin, 1905), pp. 96–100; p. 81 on the *Etat Incarnadin;* p. 87 about the *Habitués du Samedi.* In regard to Pellisson's financial role, Collas, *Jean Chapelain*, p. 305.

68. A. Adam, "La Genèse des *Précieuses ridicules*," *Revue des Sciences Humaines* (1939), p. 46.

69. Chatelain, pp. 539–43.

70. Georges Mongrédien, *Recueil des textes et des documents du XVIIème siècle relatifs à Molière* (Editions du Centre National de la Recherche Scientifique, 1965), I: *Les Précieuses ridicules* was performed at M. de Guénégaud's Hôtel de Nevers together with *L'Etourdi* on February 4, 1661 (p. 121); Molière's company went to Vaux on July 11, 1661, to perform *L'Ecole des maris*, and returned on August 15, 1661, for the première of *Les Fâcheux*, performed on August 17 (pp. 144–46).

71. Roger Lathuillère, *La Préciosité, étude historique et linguistique* (Genève: Droz, 1966), pp. 102–42.

72. Voltaire, *Le Siècle de Louis XIV* (Garnier-Flammarion, 1966), II, 51–52.

73. Ferdinand Lachèvre, *Oeuvres de Jean Dehénault* (Champion, 1922), p. 102.

74. Marcou, p. 245.

75. Mme de Sévigné, II, 662 (April 3, 1680).

76. Paul Pellisson, *Oeuvres diverses* (Paris: Didot, 1735; rpt. Geneva: Slatkine, 1971), p. 211; and Marcou, p. 352.

77. Mme de Sévigné, II, 929 (March 5, 1683).

78. V. Cherbulliez, *L'Idéal romanesque en France de 1610 à 1816* (Paris, 1911; rpt. Geneva: Slatkine, 1972), p. 65.

79. Mme de Sévigné, III, 684 (February 19, 1690).

80. L. G. Pélissier, "Lettres de Mademoiselle de Scudéry à Pierre-Daniel Huet," *Bulletin du Bibliophile et du Bibliothécaire* 1902, 153.

81. Marcou, p. 238.

82. Bosquillon, p. 322.

*Chapter Two*

1. Mme de Villedieu, *Les Désordres de l'amour*, ed. Micheline Cuénin (Geneva: Droz, 1970), p. xiii.

2. M. Magendie, *Le Roman français au XVIIème siècle de l'Astrée au Grand Cyrus* (Paris, 1932; rpt. Geneva: Slatkine, 1970): beginning *in medias res*, p. 23; conversations, p. 36; subplots, p. 111; Camus and *amitié tendre*, p. 331; portraits, p. 406.

3. Tallemant, II, 688. Bosquillon, pp. 317–18.

4. Quotations from the unpaged preface come from the first edition.

5. Clarence D. Rouillard, *The Turk in French History, Thought and Literature, 1550–1660* (Boivin, 1938), p. 644.

6. Cited in Rouillard, p. 569.

7. Mme de Genlis, *De L'Influence des femmes sur la littérature française* (Maradan, 1811), p. 99.

8. *Isabelle Grimaldi, Princesse de Monaco*, ed. E. Seillière (Editions du Monde Nouveau, 1923), p. 12.

9. Quotations from the novel are from the 1753 edition.

10. Arpad Steiner, "Calderón's *Astrólogo Fingido* in France" *Romanic Review*, 24, (1926) clearly demonstrates that Thomas Corneille's *Le Feint Astrologue* is much closer in many ways to *Ibrahim* than to Calderón. In fact, many dramatists have borrowed the subjects of their plays from works of Mlle de Scudéry, as is seen in H. C. Lancaster's *French Dramatic Literature of the Seventeenth Century*.

11. Charles Sorel, *La Bibliothèque françoise* (Compagnie des Libraires du Palais, 1664), p. 166.

12. Magendie, *La Politesse*, p. 852, on Condé and Mlle du Vigean, p. 523 on Bussy.

13. Bussy-Rabutin, *Histoire amoureuse des Gaules* (Garnier-Flammarion, 1967), p. 106.

14. N. Aronson, "Mlle de Scudéry et l'histoire romaine dans *Clélie*," *Romanische Forschungen* 88, (1976).

15. Cicero, *De Divinatione*, trans. W. A. Falconer (London: Heinemann; New York: Putnam, 1922), II, 85.

16. Livy, *History of Rome*, trans. Foster (Cambridge, Mass.: Harvard University Press, 1952), I, 169–71.

17. N. Aronson, "Plotine ou le Portrait de la Précieuse dans *Clélie*," *Papers on Seventeenth Century French Literature*, 4–5 (1976).

18. Abbé de Pure, *La Prétieuse*, ed. Emile Magne (Geneva: Droz, 1939), II, 113.

## Chapter Three

1. René Godenne, "Les Nouvelles de Mlle de Scudéry." *Revue des Sciences humaines*, XXXVII (1972), 148.

2. *La Morale du monde*, pagination faulty, indicates 319.

3. Chatelain, p. 321.

4. Perrier, p. 10.

5. Mongrédien, "Bibliographie," p. 554.

6. Mme de Lafayette, *Vie de la Princesse d'Angleterre*, ed. Marie-Thérèse Hipp (Geneva: Droz, 1967), p. xxvii. Redaction was started in 1664 or 1665.

7. Mme de Sévigné, I, 317.

8. M. Ratner, *Theory and Criticism of the Novel in France from L'Astrée to 1750* (New York: de Palma, 1938), p. 39.

9. L. Benoist, *Histoire de Versailles* (Presses Universitaires de France, 1973), pp. 29–30.

10. Cousin, II, 313.

11. Montaigne, *Journal de voyage en Italie,* ed. Maurice Rat (Classiques Garnier, n.d.), p. 9 and note 49, p. 256.

12. This very curious point is mentioned in Diogenes Laertius' *Lives and Opinions of Eminent Philosophers*, trans. R. D. Hicks (London: Heinemann; Cambridge, Mass.: Harvard University Press, 1950), I, 157.

13. Montaigne, *Essais*, ed. M. Rat, (Garnier, 1962), I, 86–88.

14. Gustave Michaut published this section of *L'Histoire du Comte*

*d'Albe* under the title *Tableau de la poésie française au XVIème siècle* (Sansot, 1907). Quotations come from this edition.

15. Marcou, p. 483.
16. Festugière, p. 141.
17. Marcou, p. 75.
18. J. E. Fidao-Justiniani, *L'Esprit classique et la préciosité au XVIIème siècle* (Picard, 1914), p. 35.

## Chapter Four

1. F. E. Sutcliffe, *Guez de Balzac et son temps: Littérature et politique* (Nizet, 1959), p. 117.
2. Montaigne, *Les Essais*, II, chap. XVI, p. 15.
3. Descartes, *Oeuvres*, ed. Ch. Adam and P. Tannery (Librairie philosophique Vrin, 1967), IX, 482, article 204.
4. C. indicates *Conversations sur divers sujets;* CN, *Conversations nouvelles sur divers sujets;* E, *Entretiens de morale;* M, *Morale du monde.*
5. Magendie, *La Politesse mondaine*, p. 305.
6. *Morale du monde,* pagination faulty, indicates 317–18.
7. Martin Lister, *A Journey to Paris in the Year 1698,* ed. Raymond P. Stearns (Urbana: University of Illinois Press), p. 96.
8. L. C. Rosenfield, *From Beast-Machine to Man-Machine* (New York: Octagon Books, 1968), pp. 159–63.
9. A. Adam, *Histoire de la littérature française,* II, 138.
10. N. Ivanoff, *Mme de Sablé et son salon* (Presses modernes, 1927), p. 144.
11. Sutcliffe, p. 255. Also see *Héroisme et création littéraire sous les règnes d'Henri IV et de Louis XIII,* ed. Noémie Hepp and Georges Livet (Klincksieck: Actes et Colloques, 1974), XVI.
12. Cited in Rosenfield, p. 163.
13. Cited in Belmont, p. 657.
14. Lachèvre, pp. 102–104.

## Chapter Five

1. Raymond Picard, *Two Centuries of French Literature,* trans. John Cairncross (New York: McGraw-Hill Book Company, 1970), p. 110.
2. Mme de Sévigné, I, 332 (July 12, 1671).
3. Furetière, *Le Roman bourgeois,* quoted in Picard, p. 111.
4. Jacquette Guillaume, *Histoire des Dames illustres,* quoted in Clerc, p. 47.

5. Clerc, p. 76; Barbara R. Woshinsky, *La Princesse de Clèves: The Tension of Elegance* (The Hague: Mouton, 1973), p. 62.

6. Mme de Sévigné, I, 135 (December 9, 1664).

7. Mme de Sévigné, II, 954 (September 11, 1684). Although Mme de Sévigné admired Mlle de Scudéry's works, it must be noted that her favorite novelist was La Calprenède.

8. La Fontaine, *Oeuvres diverses* ed. P. Clarac (Pléiade, 1958), p. 586, for the *Ballade;* p. 96, for *Le Songe de Vaux,* and P. Clarac's note, p. 820. J. P. Collinet, *Le Monde littéraire de La Fontaine* (Presses Universitaires de France, 1970) pp. 100–11 and note 480, insists on certain similarities between the works of Mlle de Scudéry and La Fontaine.

9. La Bruyère, *Oeuvres complètes,* ed. J. Benda (Pléiade, 1951), p. 348.

10. Rathery and Boutron reproduce a great number of letters showing the wide range of Mlle de Scudéry's correspondence. This is, however, far from being a complete collection of her correspondence. Many of the letters have been lost, and others are widely scattered among the works of other authors. It should be noted that her relationship with certain major writers is still badly known. This is especially evident in the case of Corneille. The playful tone of Mlle de Scudéry's poem (R, 438–39) seems to indicate that their relationship, despite Georges Couton's interpretation in *La Vieillesse de Corneille* (Maloine, n.d.), p. 98, was a close one. It can be remembered that they had certainly known each other since 1631, when Corneille published his first poem dedicated to Georges de Scudéry; see Corneille's *Oeuvres complètes,* p. 863. See also Lathuillère, pp. 458–59, and Chapter 2, note 10.

11. V. Cousin, *Jacqueline Pascal* (Didier, 1869), p. 97; V. Cousin, *Mme de Sablé* (Didier, 1869), pp. 125–29.

12. Adam, "La Préciosité," p. 39.

13. Pascal, *Oeuvres complètes,* ed. L. Lafuma (Seuil, coll. l'Intégrale, 1963), p. 379;

14. Jean Racine, *Oeuvres,* ed. Paul Mesnard (Hachette, 1886), IV, 289 and 321.

15. Cousin, *Mme de Sablé,* p. 86.

16. Victor Fournel, *La Littérature indépendante et les écrivains oubliés. Essai de critique et d'érudition sur le XVIIème siècle* (Didier, 1962), p. 172.

17. Abbé de Pure, I, 143–44.

18. Somaize, II, 135–36.

19. Huet, "Lettre sur l'origine des romans," in *Oeuvres complètes de Mesdames de La Fayette, de Tencin et de Fontaine,* ed. Jay (Moutardier, 1825), I, 72–73.

20. *Ménagiana,* pp. 224–26.

21. Sorel, pp. 162–64.

22. F. Baumal, *Molière, auteur précieux* (Renaissance du Livre, 1924);

Henri Cottez, "Molière et Mlle de Scudéry," *Revue des Sciences Humaines*, (1943); J. H. Whitfield, "A Note on Molière and Mlle de Scudéry," *Le Parole e le Idee*, 5, (1963).

23. Magendie, *La Politesse mondaine*, pp. 277 and 588; Lathuillère, pp. 143–46.

24. Molière *Sganarelle ou le cocu imaginaire* in *Oeuvres complètes* (Seuil, coll. l'Intégrale, 1962), p. 113, (verses 31–33).

25. Molière, p. 158 (verse 1062).

26. Furetière, *Le Roman bourgeois*, in *Romanciers du XVIIème siècle*, ed. A. Adam (Pléiade, 1958), p. 989.

27. Barthélémy, pp. 34, 168; Abbé Cognet, *Antoine Godeau* (Picard, 1900), p. 245, cites a very flattering letter written to Mlle de Scudéry at a later date.

28. *Lettres de Jean Chapelain*, ed. Tamizey de Larroque (Paris, 1883; rpt. Imprimerie nationale, 1968), I, 483 (Aug. 21, 1639); for Chapelain's opinion about novels, see III, 542.

29. On the relationship Gilles Boileau–Nicolas Boileau, see Adam's introduction to Nicolas Boileau, *Oeuvres complètes*, pp. xi–xii; and Gustave Lanson, *Boileau* (Hachette, 1906), pp. 14–15. About President Lamoignon's *Lundis*, see Lanson, pp. 30–31 and Adam's introduction to Boileau, pp. xv, xvii. About Brossette, see Adam, p. 917, n. 26.

30. N. Boileau, p. 21: In *Satire* III, he accepts an invitation to dinner and finds himself received by: "Deux nobles campagnards, grands lecteurs de romans/Qui m'ont dit tout *Cyrus* dans leurs longs compliments" (Two noble peasants, great readers of novels, who greeted me at great length, reciting *Cyrus* all the while).

31. N. Boileau, pp. 215–16.

32. N. Boileau, p. 67.

33. N. Boileau, p. 445.

34. Arnauld's letter is quoted in Boileau pp. 580–81.

35. La Bruyère, p. 83.

36. Bosquillon, p. 317.

37. N. Boileau, p. 445.

38. N. Boileau, p. 171.

39. N. Aronson, "Mlle de Scudéry et l'histoire romaine dans *Clélie*," p. 183.

40. Jean Chapelain, *De La Lecture des vieux romans*, ed. Alphone Feillet (Paris 1870; rpt. Genève: Slatkine, 1968), p. 12.

41. *Romanciers du XVIIème*, ed. A. Adam, p. 13. There is a very abundant bibliography on the change from the *roman héroique* to the *nouvelle* and the *histoire*. Among the numerous studies, the most important seem to be the following: Arnaldo Pizzorusso, *La Poetica del Romanzo in Francia 1660–1685* (Caltanissetta-Roma: Sciascia, 1962), p. 7, and chapter 3, "La Crisi del romanzo' eroico' e l'evoluzione della poetica del romanzo: da Mlle

de Scudéry a Segrais"; E. Showalter, *The Evolution of the French Novel, 1641–1782* (Princeton: Princeton University Press, 1972), pp. 11–37, 131–33; René Godenne, *Histoire de la nouvelle française aux 17 et 18èmes siècles* (Geneva: Droz, 1970), pp. 27–79; Henri Coulet, *Le Roman jusqu'à la Révolution* (Colin, 1967), I, 208–32; Arpad Steiner, "A French Poetics of the Novel in 1683," *Romanic Review,* 30 (1939); René Godenne, "L'Association nouvelle-petit roman entre 1650 et 1750," *Cahiers de l'Association Internationale des Etudes Françaises,* 18 (1966), 67–78; A. Kibédi Varga, "Pour une définition de la nouvelle à l'époque classique," *Cahiers de l'Association Internationale des Etudes Françaises,* 18 (1966), 53–65; Georges May, "L'Histoire a-t-elle engendré le roman?" *Revue d'Histoire Littéraire de la France,* 55 (1955).

42. Godenne, *Histoire de la nouvelle française,* p. 62, gives a list of the *nouvelles* published between 1661 and 1671.

43. A. Pizzorusso, "La Concezione dell'arte narrativa nella seconda metà del seicento francese," *Studi Mediolatini e Volgari,* 3 (1955), 115–18; and Showalter pp. 27–29.

44. Mme de Villedieu, pp. xx and 66.

45. Godenne, "L'Association nouvelle-petit roman," p. 69.

46. Georges May, *Le Dilemme du roman au XVIIIème siècle. Etude sur les rapports du roman et de la critique* (New Haven: Yale University Press, and Presses Universitaires de France, 1963), p. 21.

47. As indicated by Mornet in his abundant introduction to his edition of Rousseau's *La Nouvelle Héloise* (Hachette, 1925), I, 10.

48. J. J. Rousseau, *Les Confessions* (Garnier-Flammarion, 1968), I, 47.

49. Chateaubriand, *Les Mémoires d'Outre-Tombe* (Pléiade, 1951), p. 16.

50. Bayle, *Dictionnaire historique et critique,* (Rep. P. Desoer, 1820) mentions Mlle de Scudéry, in volume XIII, under the heading of Sapho.

51. Abbé Prévost, *Le Pour et le contre* (Didot, 1733), I, 48.

52. Voltaire, *Le Siècle de Louis XIV,* II, 283.

53. Voltaire, *Correspondance,* ed. Besterman, (Banbury, Oxfordshire: The Voltaire Foundation, 1974), vol. 118, 421.

54. Marmontel, *Essai sur les romans,* quoted in F. Vézinet, *Le XVIIème siècle vu par le XVIIIème* (Vuibert, 1924), p. 176.

55. La Harpe, *Lycée ou Cours de littérature,* quoted *Ibid.,* p. 173.

56. Cousin, *La Société française,* I, 10.

57. Barthélémy, p. 1.

58. Sainte-Beuve, *Causeries du Lundi* (Classiques Garnier), IV, 128; and *Portraits littéraires,* in *Oeuvres* (Pléiade, 1960), II, 1335.

59. Saint-Marc Girardin, *Cours de Littérature dramatique* (Charpentier, 1870), pp. 108–20.

60. E. Faguet, *Histoire de la poésie française de la Renaissance au Romantisme* (Boivin, 1927), III, 53.

61. A. Bellessort, *Heures de parole* (Librarie académique Perrin, 1929),

p. 176. The section on Mlle de Scudéry is entitled "Une Romancière européenne."

62. Addison and Steele, *The Spectator*, ed. Donald F. Bond (Oxford: Clarendon Press, 1965), I, 154–56, 218; II, 437.

63. *The Diary of Samuel Pepys*, ed. Henry B. Wheatley (London: G. Bell, 1952), I, 280; V, 272; VII, 315; VIII, 51.

64. *The Plays of Richard Steele*, ed. Shirley Strum Kenny (Oxford: Clarendon Press, 1971), p. 258. See also p. 223.

65. Sir Walter Scott, *The Life of John Dryden*, ed. Bernard Kreissman (Lincoln: University of Nebraska Press, 1963), p. 59.

66. Lister, p. 96.

67. E. T. A. Hoffmann, *Werke*, ed. Gisela Spiekerkötter (Zurich: Stauffacher-Verlag, 1965), IV, 321–77.

# Selected Bibliography

BIBLIOGRAPHIES

CABEEN, DAVID C., and JULES BRODY, ed. *A Critical Bibliography of French Literature.* Vol. III: *The Seventeenth Century,* ed. Nathan Edelman. Syracuse, N.Y.: Syracuse University Press, 1961.

CIORANESCU, ALEXANDRE. *Bibliographie de la littérature française du dix-septième siècle.* Vol. II. Editions du Centre National de la Recherche Scientifique, 1966.

PRIMARY SOURCES

*Ibrahim ou L'Illustre Bassa.* 4 vols. Sommaville, 1641. The quotations come from P. Witte's 1723 edition. Since it does not include the preface, that part is taken from the 1641 edition.

*Ibrahim or the Illustrious Bassa, an Excellent New Romance,* Fol. Trans. Henry Cogan. London: J. R., 1652.

*Isabelle Grimaldi, Princesse de Monaco.* Ed. E. Seillière. Aux Editions du Monde Nouveau, 1923. An abridged edition of *Ibrahim* containing only the main plot.

*Les Femmes illustres ou Les Harangues héroiques.* Part I: Sommaville et Courbé, 1642. Part II: Quinet et de Sercy, 1644.

*Artamène ou Le Grand Cyrus.* 10 vols. Courbé, 1649–1653. The quotations are from the Slatkine reprint of the Paris 1646 edition, Geneva, 1972.

*Artamenes, or The Grand Cyrus, an Excellent New Romance.* Fol. Trans. F. G. London, 1653–1655.

*Clélie, Histoire romaine.* 10 vols. Courbé, 1654–1660. The quotations come from the Slatkine reprint of the 1660 edition, Geneva, 1973.

*Clelia, An Excellent New Romance.* Trans. J. Davies and Havers. 1656–1661. Another edition. London, 1678.

*Célinte, Nouvelle première.* Courbé, 1661.

*Mathilde* d'Aguilar. Martin et Eschart, 1667.

*La Promenade de Versailles.* Barbin, 1669.

*Discours sur la gloire.* Le Petit, 1671.

171

*An Essay upon Glory.* Trans. by a person of the same sex. London, 1708.

*Conversations sur divers sujets.* 2 vols. Barbin, 1680.

*Conversations upon Several Subjects.* 2 vols. Trans. F. Spence. London, 1683.

*Conversations nouvelles sur divers sujets.* 2 vols. Barbin, 1684.

*De la poésie françoise jusques à Henry Quatriesme.* Ed. Gustave Michaut. Sansot, 1907. An excerpt from one of the *Conversations.*

*Conversations morales ou La Morale du monde.* 2 vols. 1686. Quotations are from the Amsterdam edition of 1688.

*Nouvelles conversations de morale.* 2 vols. Cramoisy, 1688.

*Entretiens de morale.* 2 vols. Jean Anisson, 1692.

Mlle de Scudéry's printed poems are scattered throughout the *recueils,* such as *Recueil de Sercy* or *Recueil La Suze-Pellisson.* For a listing, see Georges Mongrédien, "Bibliographie des oeuvres de Georges et Madeleine de Scudéry," *Revue d'Histoire Littéraire de la France,* 40 (1933).

### SECONDARY SOURCES

A. General

ADAM, ANTOINE. *Histoire de la littérature française au XVIIème siècle.* 5 vols. Del Duca, 1958. Basic text for the study of any seventeenth century subject matter.

―――――. "Baroque et Préciosité." *Revue des Sciences Humaines,* 53, (Janvier–Mars 1949).

―――――. "La Préciosité." *Cahiers de l'Association des Etudes françaises,* 1 (1959). Indispensable articles on the meaning of *Préciosité* and its manifestations.

BELMONT, LOUIS. "Documents inédits sur la société et la littérature précieuses: extraits de la chronique du samedi, publiés d'après le registre original de Pellisson (1652–1657)." *Revue d'histoire littéraire de la France,* 9 (October-December 1902). Selections from the *Chronique du Samedi.*

CHARLIER, GUSTAVE. "La fin de l'Hôtel de Rambouillet." *Revue Belge de Philosophie et d'Histoire,* 18 (1939). A refutation of Roederer's theory.

COLOMBEY, EMILE. *La Journée des madrigaux.* Aubry, 1856. A collection of texts written on that famous day, followed by *La Gazette de Tendre.*

COTTEZ, HENRI. "Molière et Mlle de Scudéry." *Revue des Sciences Humaines* (1943). Negates any connection between Mlle de Scudéry and *Les Précieuses ridicules* or *Les Femmes savantes,* and shows her influence on Molière.

KOERTING, HEINRICH. *Geschichte des Französischen Romans im XVII Jahhundert.* Oppeln and Leipzig: Franck, 1891. Although inaccurate on a few points, good insight into Mlle de Scudéry's works. However, preferred La Calprenède.

LATHUILLÈRE, ROGER. *La Préciosité, étude historique et linguistique.* Geneva: Droz, 1966. Exhaustive study of *Préciosité* and its manifestations. Excellent comments on Mlle de Scudéry.

McGILLIVRAY, RUSSELL. "La Préciosité: essai de mise au point." *Revue des Sciences Humaines,* 105 (1962). Another definition of *Préciosité,* mentioning the importance of humor.

MAGNE, EMILE. *Voiture et les origines de l'Hôtel de Rambouillet.* Mercure de France, 1911.

————. *Voiture et les années de gloire de l'Hôtel de Rambouillet:* Emile-Paul, 1930. Both of Magne's works give an excellent description of the milieu that nurtured Mlle de Scudéry's development.

MAGENDIE, MAURICE. *La Politesse mondaine et les théories de l'honnêteté en France au XVIIème, de 1600 à 1660.* Alcan, 1925; rpt. Geneva: Slatkine, 1970. Complete study of French seventeenth century *vie de société,* with a well-documented chapter on *Cyrus* and *Clélie.*

PIZZORUSSO, ARNALDO. *La Poetica del Romanzo in Francia 1660–1685.* Caltanissetta-Rome: Sciascia, 1962. Excellent study of seventeenth century novels and their evolution after 1660.

WHITFIELD, J. H. "A Note on Molière and Mlle de Scudéry." *Le Parole e le Idee,* 5 (1963). Shows that Molière borrowed material from Mlle de Scudéry's novels, and calls for a reevaluation of her works, especially *Clélie.*

B. Works dealing with Mlle de Scudéry

ARAGONNÈS, CLAUDE. *Madeleine de Scudéry, Reine du Tendre.* Colin, 1934. Valuable mostly for the description of Mlle de Scudéry's friends.

BARTHÉLÉMY, EDOUARD DE. *Sapho, le mage de Sidon et Zénocrate, étude sur la société précieuse d'après des lettres inédites de mademoiselle de Scudéry, de Godeau et d'Isarn.* Didier, 1880. A study of the *Précieux* utilizing letters from Mlle de Scudéry, Godeau, and Isarn.

BARTHÉLÉMY, EDOUARD DE, AND RENE KERVILER. *Un Tournoi de trois Pucelles.* Picard, 1878. Collection of correspondence between Mlle de Scudéry, Mlle du Moulin, Conrart, and Rivet on the subject of Joan of Arc.

BELLESSORT, ANDRE. *Heures de parole.* Librairie académique Perrin, 1929. Text of a lecture demonstrating a deep understanding of Mlle de Scudéry.

BOSQUILLON. "Eloge de Mlle de Scudéry." *Journal des Savants,* July 11, 1701. Evaluation of Mlle de Scudéry and her works by a contemporary.

COUSIN, VICTOR. *La Société française au XVIIème siècle d'après Le Grand Cyrus.* Perrin, 1905. This book was responsible for rescuing Mlle de Scudéry from oblivion.

GODENNE, RENE. "Les Nouvelles de Mlle de Scudéry." *Revue des Sciences humaines* XXXVII, 148, (October-December 1972). Asserts that the three short stories published independently were actually *"petits romans."*

MCDOUGALL, DOROTHY. *Madeleine de Scudéry, Her Romantic Life and Death.* London: Methuen, 1938. Heretofore the only book on Mlle de Scudéry published in English.

MAGNE, EMILE. *Le Salon de Mlle de Scudéry ou Le Royaume de Tendre.* Monaco: Société des Conférences, 1927. Magne has been able in these few pages to show his total understanding of the *Samedi.*

MONGRÉDIEN, GEORGES. *Madeleine de Scudéry et son salon.* Tallandier, 1946. A scholarly study that often assumes a rather mocking tone.

NIDERST, ALAIN. *Madeleine de Scudéry, Paul Pellisson et leur monde.* Presses Universitaires de France, 1976. The latest French study of the historical setting in which Mlle de Scudéry and her friends lived.

RATHERY AND BOUTRON. *Mademoiselle de Scudéry; Sa vie et sa correspondance.* Téchener, 1873. Despite certain inaccuracies, this is still the basic study on Mlle de Scudéry. Contains a selection of letters and poems.

SANTA CELORIA, RITA. *Le grand Cyrus, Clélie: Episodes choisis avec le résumé des deux romans.* Turin: Giappichelli, 1973. Contains lengthy excerpts from *Cyrus* and *Clélie.* Good introduction, although the connection made between Mlle de Scudéry and the *baroque* can be questioned.

STEINER, ARPAD. "Les Idées esthétiques de Mlle de Scudéry." *Romanic Review,* 16 (1925). Appraisal of Mlle de Scudéry's ideas on novels.

C. Unpublished Dissertations: Scholarly studies of the subjects involved. Dr. Nunn's work on *Clélie* is of special interest.

AUBE, LUCIEN. "Aspects of Reality in the *Grand Cyrus* of Madeleine de Scudéry." Dissertation, Case Western Reserve, 1970.

CISON, SISTER BARBARA. "The Samedis of Mlle de Scudéry." Dissertation, Fordham, 1967.

KEATING, REBECCA. "The Literary Portraits in the Novels of Mlle de Scudéry." Dissertation, Yale, 1970.

NUNN, ROBERT. "Mlle de Scudéry's *Clélie.*" Dissertation, Columbia, 1966.

WILSON, LAWRENCE. "The *Cyrus* and the *Clélie* of Mlle de Scudéry as Reflections of XVIIth Century Life, Ideas and Manners." Dissertation, Minnesota, 1941.

# Index